"There's a place of intimacy with th[e Lord] for the bride of Christ. In *Fully Know[n]* [...] Scripture, personal struggles, and the analogy of marriage to help guide you into experiencing greater depths of intimacy with God that we all desire to know."

Lisa Bevere, *New York Times* bestselling author
and cofounder of Messenger International

"This book is a bold and Spirit-breathed invitation into deep intimacy with the One who longs to heal us and make us whole. Mo powerfully unpacks how the layers and depths of physical intimacy actually reveal to us greater depths of the full gospel story—a lifelong journey that is often hard but always holy. This message is for everyone!"

Rebekah Lyons, bestselling author of *Rhythms*
of Renewal and *You Are Free*

"Whether you're exploring God for the first time or you've been following Jesus all your life, *Fully Known* will help you better understand the single most important aspect of your life, your identity, and your eternity, which is being fully known and loved by God. Most people go through life feeling uncertain of their worth and their purpose when God is inviting us to live life rooted in His love and presence in perfect intimacy. Mo Aiken's masterful book invites readers on a journey of discovery that will undoubtedly enrich your faith and serve as a healing balm for your weary soul. It's not an overstatement to say that this book could quite literally change your life."

Dave and Ashley Willis, authors of *The Naked Marriage*
and hosts of *The Naked Marriage* podcast

"The unapologetic call to know and be known by God in a culture desperate and wounded from our own idolatry crisis is what Mo Aiken brings to this world and this book. Through the noise God is making His voice heard, loud and clear: *I am what you want.* Mo's single focus on Him continually drives me there. You won't waste a single minute reading these inspired words."

Lisa Whittle, bestselling author of *Jesus Over Everything*, podcast host, and Bible teacher

"Are you restless? Dissatisfied? Questioning? Hungry? Thirsting for more of God yet at the same time wondering, *How do I bridge this gap?* Mo states, 'You have everything available to you that you need for a vibrant, healthy, restored, and radical relationship with the One True God,' but do we truly believe it? And more importantly, do we know how to live it? This book is a beautiful invitation to surrender into the arms of truth and love incarnate. It's a book of the pursuit of the One who has already pursued you with His entire life. Mo's passion and urgency for you to hear, turn, and run into the arms of the Father seep out of every page. If there was ever a book for the hour we find ourselves in, this is the one."

Andi Andrew, wife, mom, church planter, speaker, and author of *She Is Free* and *Fake or Follower*

"Christian bookshelves are filled with helpful resources on sex, dating, marriage, and healing written out of each author's personal experience and expertise. This book is different. As I read it, I had the sense that the words didn't come from Mo's personal thoughts but passed through her. This book contains profound spiritual truths few have been willing to plumb and receive. If your soul is weary from shallow fixes for your deep loneliness and brokenness, this book is for you. Be warned . . . God will convict you, not to pour on shame but to perform a surgery of the heart that will ultimately invite you into a greater freedom than you can even imagine. Be courageous, friend, and go on the beautiful journey Mo has set before us to be *Fully Known*."

Dr. Juli Slattery, cofounder of Authentic Intimacy and author of *Rethinking Sexuality*

"I felt this was the sort of book that I wanted to read one page (or even one paragraph) of, then go away for a while to fully reflect on it before moving on. I found myself rereading sentences and paragraphs so I could fully grasp the depth and richness being communicated. It challenged me to the core, provoking me to reexamine what it really means to follow Jesus. In a Christian culture that prefers to paddle in the shallow end of the pool, this book is a prophetic and timely wake-up call to plunge into the depths of true intimacy with Christ. Only there can we find the true satisfaction for our souls we are looking and longing for in so many other places. Sexuality, repentance, holiness, intimacy, surrender, submission, fruitfulness, and so many other key biblical themes are interwoven and integrated to paint a stirring picture of what authentic, abundant life in Christ can look like. What life in Christ *should* look like. It's a book that most Christian authors would be too scared to write. I applaud you."

Craig Cooney, lead pastor of Hope Church in N. Ireland, author of *The Tension of Transition*, *Spirit Speak*, and *I Hear Yahweh*, and curator of Instagram account @daily.prophetic

"This book is an invitation to the *more* we're all longing for. I had that well-recognized feeling of, 'these words were written just for me!' I couldn't put my highlighter down, and I believe they will be highlighted on my spirit. So thankful for Mo sharing her journey with the Lord to help lead the rest of us into the intimacy we always hoped was possible. She takes us on a journey of learning to abide rather than trying to achieve at doing the 'right' thing. It's both powerful and a bit painful to read as you have your own revelatory moments over these pages."

Caitlin Zick, codirector of *Moral Revolution* and author of *Look at You, Girl*

fully
known

fully known

An Invitation to True Intimacy with God

MO AIKEN

BakerBooks

a division of Baker Publishing Group
Grand Rapids, Michigan

Published by Baker Books
a division of Baker Publishing Group
PO Box 6287, Grand Rapids, MI 49516-6287
www.bakerbooks.com

Printed in the United States of America

Library of Congress Cataloging-in-Publication Data
Names: Aiken, Mo, 1989– author.
Title: Fully known : an invitation to true intimacy with God / Mo Aiken.
Description: Grand Rapids, Michigan : Baker Books, a division of Baker Publishing
    Group, [2021]
Identifiers: LCCN 2020042359 | ISBN 9781540900258 (paperback) | ISBN
    9781540901453 (casebound)
Subjects: LCSH: Spirituality—Christianity. | Intimacy (Psychology)—Religious
    aspects—Christianity. | God (Christianity)—Knowableness.
Classification: LCC BV4501.3 .A3855 2021 | DDC 248—dc23
LC record available at https://lccn.loc.gov/2020042359

Published in association with William K. Jensen Literary Agency.

21 22 23 24 25 26 27   7 6 5 4 3 2 1

For all those who hunger and thirst for more.

contents

introduction

Let me start by sharing a truth your heart is likely longing to be reminded of . . .

You were made to know intimacy with God.

You were created to commune with your Creator.

Tuned to know the sound of the Good Shepherd's voice.

Designed to experience His dignifying touch.

And sculpted by Him to house His perfect and powerful Spirit.

You. You are who He loves. And God has made a way for you to know Him and be known by Him both now and forevermore.

It's this very thing that sets the gospel of Jesus Christ apart in a sea of man-made religions, ideologies, theories, and cults. It is, in fact, what makes a life in Christ distinctly different from the worship of every false god and every mockery of the true faith that labels itself as "Christian." While every other religion hinges on people's ability to work their hardest to ascend to God, the Good News of Yeshua (the Hebrew name for Jesus) is that God Himself has descended to us. The Maker of the heavens and the earth, the Alpha and Omega, the One who was and is and is to come—He came into the company of the rebels and wanderers, the sick and suffering, the unclean sinners like you and me, and brought both dignity and divinity into our midst. He came to us and called us His own. And by believing in Him and the truth about Him—that He was God in the flesh—we are not only freed from our enslavement to sin but also encounter our true identity and are invited into an intimate relationship unlike any connection we've ever known. We are offered oneness, intimate and passionate oneness, with the One who made us. A oneness that transforms us, restores us, and empowers us to do His will.

So, if intimacy with God Almighty is freely offered to us through the Savior we claim to love, why do we, as professed believers, often feel so far from God? Where is the disconnect?

Is there anything we can learn about intimacy with God through the physical model of intimacy He has given us?

This book serves as my best effort to answer those very questions. Because I too found myself in a season of faith where I was wrestling with Scriptures I didn't understand, fighting feelings of discouragement and disqualification, and ultimately feeling unfathomably far from the God I loved and longed to serve.

But in the midst of my deepest valley, He came to me and called me His own. Yet again. He heard my cries, had compassion on my confused heart, and ultimately gifted me with revelation that changed everything. He gave me eyes to see more of His nature and His great design of intimacy like I never had before, pouring out prophetic understanding that has transformed both my spiritual and my physical life.

And I now feel pregnant with purpose. Brimming with great expectation and joy. I wholeheartedly believe that some of the revelation and understanding about intimacy He opened my eyes to has the power to transform your life as well. I believe through this message, by the grace of God, He will bring revival to hearts, restoration to homes, and resurrected spiritual intimacy to every member of the body of Christ who longs to know Him more.

But before we dive into dissecting some of God's design and investigating what He has unveiled about intimacy with Him, there

14

are several things I want to say in a very blunt fashion. Primarily because I, personally, benefit most when those who love me teach hard truths in the same way.

These pages seek to fill you with beauty, clarity, invitation, and tender grace. But they also hold many matter-of-fact, unapologetic, and hard pills to swallow. There are a few gut punches and strong reprimands along the way, several portions that may cause you to pause, and searing sections that may prod unhealed wounds. I assure you this is all for your good and His glory, so I hope you'll stay. Even when it's easier to run, stay.

Know that I love you. I don't know you, most likely. But I know that you're an image-bearing creation of God who carries immeasurable worth, value, and purpose no matter what season of life you're in or sin struggle you're wrestling through. You were made by the Creator, whom I love, and His works are wonderful; my soul knows that very well (Ps. 139:14). He loves you, so I love you. And I want nothing more than for you to walk forward in the fullness of truth, covered by His grace and filled with His perfect Holy Spirit.

Since I love Him, and love you, it's my job to accurately communicate with you in the fullness of biblical love. Not the self-serving, feel-good, pleasure-based lust lorded by emotion that we call "love" but genuine, Christlike love. Love that is both affectionate yet unwaveringly absolute in nature. Love that carries both delight and discipline, comfort and conviction, healing and hard accountability. Love that values the state of your eternity more than your momentary comfort.

True love. That is the goal of my heart in these words. So here goes.

◦ ◉ ◉ ◉ ◦

I am finding, more and more, that one of our greatest struggles within the body of professed believers is our deep lack of personal relationship with the Lord. We say those words often, "Oh, it's relationship, not religion," yet many hearts are wholly hypocritical in living out of that truth. We look to religion and the religious institution for all of our answers and all of our "intimacy." We know the voice and opinions of our favorite pastors and "Christian influencers" better than we know the voice of the Good Shepherd. We would rather watch a highlight reel on Instagram than hole up with His presence. We would prefer to work ourselves to the bone in the name of "service to the kingdom" in hopes those labors will prove to others and God that we are all in. (Trust me, I know from experience on that one!) We feast on the fast food of self-motivation and self-empowerment that others dole out, chasing a spiritual high rather than committing to abiding intimacy with God. We flock to pulpits that are occupied by motivational talks rather than movements of the Spirit. And we line our bookshelves with the paperback opinions of creative authors while His Word collects dust on our bedside tables. We praise the Jesus we've sculpted in our own image rather than the Jesus of the Bible. And we raise our hands to worship music, if it lives up to our taste and has a catchy build, rather than allowing our imperfect praise to build a throne for the Almighty in our midst.

We know a lot about God, but we don't truly know God.

It's no wonder we feel disconnected, disheartened, and void of true intimacy.

You know how babies deprived of touch and interaction fail to thrive and oftentimes die? I wonder if our souls are suffering the same fate. We earnestly want to know God and be known by God, but we are looking to everyone and everything apart from God Himself to find Him. Why?

I hope that in picking up this book to better understand true intimacy with God, you are not solely looking to my words instead of *His*, as if I will have an answer you could not access on your own in His presence. Because that is a lie.

There is no hidden mystery for the one hungering for righteousness. There is no secret knowledge withheld from the pure heart thirsting for Living Water. I want to challenge you to stop right now and reflect on why it is you feel others have an answer you can't seem to find. Is it laziness in your "faith walk"? Insecurity? Inherited religion void of a personal indwelling of the Holy Spirit? Shame? Fear? Abuse you have endured under the thumb of other authority figures in your life?

What rests at the root of your restlessness?

The same God who graciously provided me the revelation and understanding that fill the pages of this book is the One who calls you His. You have everything available to you that you need for a vibrant, healthy, restored, and radical relationship with the One True God—the finished work of Christ, the offer of the Holy Spirit, and the living and active Word of truth.

In fact, if you continue to open and press into that Word, you will find Scripture after Scripture that affirms these very truths.

> The anointing that you received from him abides in you, and you have no need that anyone should teach you. But as his anointing teaches you about everything, and is true, and is no lie—just as it has taught you, abide in him. (1 John 2:27)

> For this is the covenant that I will make with the house of Israel after those days, declares the LORD: I will put my law within them, and I will write it on their hearts. And I will be their God, and they shall be my people. And no longer shall each one teach his neighbor and each his brother, saying, "Know the LORD," for they shall all know me, from the least of them to the greatest, declares the LORD. (Jer. 31:33–34)

> Now we have received not the spirit of the world, but the Spirit who is from God, that we might understand the things freely given us by God. (1 Cor. 2:12)

But the Helper, the Holy Spirit, whom the Father will send in my name, he will teach you all things and bring to your remembrance all that I have said to you. (John 14:26)

It is my prayer you would know that the Maker of the heavens and the earth has made Himself available to you. I pray that as you move forward in pursuit of greater intimacy with Him, you would not be like the foolish ones who failed to understand Christ's parables but rather like those He called blessed—those who had faith to believe He would make Himself known to all who cared to find Him. As Jesus said,

To you it has been given to know the secrets of the kingdom of heaven, but to them it has not been given. For to the one who has, more will be given, and he will have an abundance, but from the one who has not, even what he has will be taken away. This is why I speak to them in parables, because seeing they do not see, and hearing they do not hear, nor do they understand. Indeed, in their case the prophecy of Isaiah is fulfilled that says:

"'You will indeed hear but never understand,
    and you will indeed see but never perceive.'
For this people's heart has grown dull,
    and with their ears they can barely hear,
    and their eyes they have closed,
lest they should see with their eyes
    and hear with their ears
and understand with their heart
    and turn, and I would heal them."

But blessed are your eyes, for they see, and your ears, for they hear. For truly, I say to you, many prophets and righteous people longed to see what you see, and did not see it, and to hear what you hear, and did not hear it. (Matt. 13:11–17)

I want to make it profoundly clear that I, as a person, hold no authority over you. We all, individually and corporately, come under the pure and perfect authority of Christ. And yes, in His Word He also designates structures of earthly order and steward-ship, and certainly of marital structure, which I am not seeking to negate. But I am seeking to dismantle the idolatry and apathy that have a grip on so many and cause them to not pursue intimacy with God individually as well.

I am not seminary educated; I am not ordained or entitled to some grand position of authority in the mega-institution we've somehow made of the church. I am simply a young woman made in the image of my Father who encountered His great grace after years of eating disorders, self-harm, horrific life circumstances such as the suicide of my dad, prideful seasons of earthly success, depression, anxiety, promiscuity, trauma, and counterfeit faith. I came into revelation of my sin and my need for salvation, and I repented with a reverent heart. I was overwhelmed and indwelled by the Holy Spirit of God and have moved forward from there in a dynamic and delightful journey of faith. I continue to recognize, repent, and receive more and more revelation of Him day in and day out.

That's really it. My dog peed on our rug this morning and I am usually elbow-deep in diaper changes and tiny toddler clothes. There is nothing unique or inaccessible about my life or my words. All I bring you is an ever-growing submission to God's Word, God's will, and God's grace. I have a lot to learn, but I hope, if anything, that is encouraging to you and shows you the true na-ture of the gospel—that when we strip back all of the pomp and circumstance and degrees and titles that are merely man-made additions to the simplicity of truth, we learn that intimacy with Him is available to every single one of us . . . right now . . . today. On earth as it is and will be in heaven.

I am a follower and a messenger, a daughter with deep urgency burning in my bones to point you to the Father that you may become a true child of God too. Not because of my words but because He, alone, reveals Himself to you as you personally seek

Him. Test everything I say in these pages. Weigh my words against Scripture. Take what's offered here to Him, please. Don't put your trust in me—passionately pursue Him, and He will lead you in the way you should go.

Read these pages with an honest heart. Pray God would make Himself real, rich, and clear to you as you begin each chapter. When He answers, as I know the Father will, you will receive a taste of His sweet manna that cultivates your appetite for true intimacy. Intimacy that is intoxicating, soul-shifting, and transformational. Ask, and you will be answered. Seek, and you will find. Press forward in a right-postured pursuit, and you may just discover the One you've been longing for is sitting at your well, waiting by your side.

Heavenly Father,

I love You. I thank You for who You are. You are mighty, holy, and just. You are full of authority, strength, sovereignty, and power. And, in the same breath, You are tender, kind, patient, and full of love. Hallowed be Your name. You know every hair on my head; You knit me together in my mother's womb. Thank You for seeing me. Thank You for meeting me right where I am and for communing with me. As I read through these pages, I pray You will speak. I pray You will translate each and every word to my spirit. You know every detail of my story and every circumstance in my life. Please give me understanding and please allow my faith to rise. When I have doubts and questions, strengthen my faith to prevail over my fear. Anoint my head with oil and bless me with revelation. Open my eyes; give me ears to hear and a heart to receive. I long for Your will to be done above all. I long to know and surrender to Your ways. Bind up my pride, in Jesus's name. Please, Lord, give me humility and wisdom as I digest these words. I know You will not withhold

humility and wisdom from those who earnestly seek You, so I pray You will pour out these gifts of Your character into my heart. I pray, in the power of Jesus's name, that You will protect me as I press through these pages. I rebuke any and all efforts of the enemy to confuse, deceive, distract, or discourage me. No weapon formed against me, as I draw near to You and Your heart, will stand. I pray the blood of Jesus, of Yeshua, over myself and over the spaces I will occupy as I read in the days ahead. Thank You, God, for Your great invitation. I exalt and bless Your name.
   Amen.

the agitation

When you stand before the Lord, what will you hear?

Are you *sure*?

At the core of the human condition, I believe one of the greatest longings of our heart is to be sure of our eternity. To know, in the end, when that last breath leaves our lungs, we won't have misunderstood and missed the mark. That we won't have wasted our days or been deceived along the way. That we will have *truly* lived a life full of faith, love, stewardship, and purpose. And we want to know that when we stand before the Lord, He will receive us and that our eternity will be spent in His perfect presence.

But Matthew 7:21–23 makes it quite clear that not all who call Christ "Lord" will be saved.

That many will stand before Him and be turned away.

Wait, what?

> Not everyone who says to me, "Lord, Lord," will enter the kingdom of heaven, but the one who does the will of my Father who is in heaven. On that day many will say to me, "Lord, Lord, did we not prophesy in your name, and cast out demons in your name, and do many mighty works in your name?" And then will I declare to

them, "I never knew you; depart from me, you workers of lawlessness." (Matt. 7:21–23)

I remember first coming across this Scripture when I was younger in the faith. I brushed past it quickly—sweeping the words to the side, self-righteously certain they were not applicable to me. If I had never heard any teaching about them in church, then they must not be that significant to the gospel story. I chose not to wrestle with them, because, ultimately, it's often easier to avoid what confuses us. To simply trek over ground that truly needs excavating. It takes concerted effort to concern ourselves with matters of great measure. And, truthfully, the words in my Bible that I didn't understand often pulsed a wave of fear through me.

So I dodged that passage—along with many others—for many years.

It's interesting . . . our deepest longings are to be *sure*, yet we'll settle quickly for *feeling safe* if the exploration of truth challenges our comfort. Isaiah 30:8–11 reveals the heart of humanity quite unapologetically: we are stubborn rebels who loathe discomfort. We would often prefer to hang the hope of our eternity on lies that satisfy our emotions rather than truth that saves our souls.

We claim to want to live bold, courageous, and confident lives of faith, but we often fight with and run from the harder callings and the harder questions because, at the core, our human nature prefers "neutral." "Just enough" feels more palatable when the just nature of God is intimidating to explore. Lukewarm is appealing when our sinful flesh is sensitive to extremes. But does God not make His thoughts clear on that condition in Revelation 3:16? No, we usually prefer to fall back to what we know and like: comfortable, cultural Christianity. After all, religion is the thick robe we often hide our raw selves behind.

Rather than wrestling with His words and petitioning Him for understanding, I simply pressed forward. I boldly professed my faith in the Lord, gave what I knew of my heart to give, and did my best to serve the kingdom without ceasing. I worked and worked and worked for the cause of Christ. Late nights and early mornings. Flights and drives and travel far and wide. I penned books and spoke on stages. Fielded emails, calls, and interviews. I worshiped at the golden calf of my iPhone, serving social media with every word and revelation and encouragement I discovered. I prayed bold prayers for miracles and healing and hope for all who needed such petition. I laid down my life in matrimony, surrendered my body in childbearing, juggled every task and deadline and motherly to-do as best as I knew how. I worked and worked and worked unto the Lord . . .

Until the day I looked up and realized the intimate presence of the Lord was nowhere to be found.

I was working unto myself. And I was completely burned out.

I remember sitting in the dark of my daughter's bedroom one night, and the culmination of my "going," my fatigue, and my frustration overwhelmed me. I whimpered, "God, where are You? Have You somehow departed from me? You told me You would never leave me nor forsake me, but somehow in the midst of living for You, I miss You. Have I *missed* You?"

From all I had previously known and all I had been churched to believe, the questions I was crying out seemed foolish. I had been *doing* fruitful, faithful, and full things, yet somehow, as I came up for air, I felt distant from the One whose name I prayed all of those works glorified. I couldn't deny how I felt. I was ten years into following Christ and somehow this separation, this feeling of desperate distance from God, was suddenly very real and very heavy. My spirit felt burdened and my heart wrenched within me. How could this be?

It was then that Matthew 7:21–23 echoed in my mind. I found myself fragile (more fragile than I would care to confess) as the living and active Word pierced through me (Heb. 4:12) and began to divide my fleshly want for comfort from my spiritual need for clarity.

I never KNEW you . . .

The words were deeply, deeply agitating. And they certainly weren't what I wanted to hear the day I stood before God, so it disturbed me that they were all I heard echoing through my mind for days, weeks, months. This entire passage of Scripture sat like a weight on my chest. It rested like a puzzle before me, dust atop its scattered pieces. It was a puzzle that had been patiently waiting for me to acknowledge it: to pick it up, investigate every portion and part, and put it together.

I knew 2 Timothy 3:16–17 to be true, that "All Scripture is breathed out by God and profitable for teaching, for reproof, for correction, and for training in righteousness, that the [messenger] of God may be complete, equipped for every good work." So even though it was uncomfortable at face value, I had to believe that particular line—more specifically, that one word, *knew*—served as a corner piece imperative to my understanding. Key to the fullness of the puzzle's image taking shape.

But what did all this *mean*?

How could one possibly call Christ "Lord" yet not be received?

Can we *call* Him Lord without actually *knowing* Him as Lord?

What is the will of the Father in heaven?

In Matthew 7, those before Him cry back to Him describing the miraculous works they did in Christ's name . . . all they did *for* the Lord . . . yet they are still dismissed.

Are our fruitful works not the fullness of His will?

Can we be working for the Lord yet miss Him entirely?

And could many of our efforts ultimately be works of lawlessness?

If, in light of everything, reception into the kingdom of heaven hangs in the balance of knowing and being known by God, then what does that *mean*?

To know Him. To be known by Him. Truly.

Those words wound themselves through my heart and reminded me, with each pulse, that my uncertainty and insecurity meant there were gaps in my understanding of His glory. That the perverse fear welling up when I read through His Word was evidence His perfect love had not yet been made complete in me (1 John 4:18). No, there was *more* of God, and it was imperative I investigate. And if the state of my eternity was woven together with rightly understanding His words, then this exploration was expected of me. Just as it's expected of you.

After all, 2 Corinthians 13:5 reminds us to "Examine yourselves, to see whether you are in the faith. Test yourselves. Or do you not realize this about yourselves, that Jesus Christ is in you?—unless indeed you fail to meet the test!"

Sure, it would have been easier to just run. To just stop caring, stop thinking so deeply about it, stop digging into the depths that brought discomfort. It would have been easier to just numb it. To distract myself with mindless entertainment, to keep myself busy with work, to suppress the conviction of the Holy Spirit urging me to care. But something about His Word presented itself as an oddly packaged invitation. It coaxed me into its company, even in the midst of my confusion.

I truly believe there are moments in all our walks of faith when God allows for deeply unsettling angst, tension, and conflict in our spirits. When He orchestrates encounters with parts of His Word or His nature or His ways that disrupt all we thought we knew. Moments when He allows for elements of our belief structure that once seemed light and clear to feel heavy and clouded. When He prompts our minds to call into question the theology we've always hung our hat on. When He invites us to weigh the countless words we've heard regurgitated from popular pulpits. Moments when He ultimately calls us to take accountability for our own faith. And to seek Him for the answers that evade our own understanding.

My encounter with this Scripture was one of those moments for me. And while I admittedly feared what I might find when I drew near to His Word, what He unveiled to me was a gift of revelation that changed everything.

To Know

I never knew you.

The line continued to echo through my mind as my restlessness truly rooted on that simple word: *know*. There was a weight to it, as if the whole of my understanding of the passage hung on its right interpretation. And what stood out to me most was that it seemed to have very little to do with the efforts and labors of those pleading their cause.

Clearly the parable was speaking of those who, at bare minimum, acknowledged Jesus Christ as Lord with their lips and, likely, their minds. And it would seem as though they had committed some portion of their lives to serving God and carried some degree of spiritual authority, as they argued all they had *done* for the Lord. Miraculous and powerful works, even! They pleaded He pay attention to what they had produced, that He take into account their work. Yet still He dismissed them as strangers—workers of lawlessness, even—who had misunderstood what was most important along the way. They utilized His name for labor and gain but somehow they missed being *known* by God.

The thought was disconcerting, as I resonated deeply with the subjects of the story. When and where these words found me, I likely would have argued the same. In so many ways I was a goer and doer. An achiever and worker. To some degree, aren't we all?

◦ ◉ ◉ ◉ ◦

We long to be acknowledged. To be seen. To have a place and a purpose in the world. To be loved and received. So, we busy ourselves with service and applaudable efforts and vain pursuits and a calendar that mocks the model of rhythmic rest. We perform for the applause of others, saying yes to every opportunity set before us. We put on a pretty face, trying to ensure that people see only the version of us we've had time to doll up. We commit our time and energy and effort to convincing ourselves and others we are capable of doing it all, though behind closed doors we're wearing thin and feeling far from the One we claim we are living for.

It's not that our intentions are all bad. In fact, many times, we're earnest-hearted and sacrificial in the assignments we take on. But if you are anywhere near the place I was, you're tired. Disconnected. Unsatisfied. And it's hard to deny, in your heart of hearts, that something is off. Something is missing. Though the *more* your soul longs for seems hard to identify.

In our efforts to *do*, we've either forgotten or diminished how to simply *be*. And it's negatively affected most every area of our lives.

But if there's one thing I've come to learn about God's nature, it is this: He is absolutely intentional. Clear. Unchanging and precise. He makes Himself explicitly available. Those who seek Him, find (Deut. 4:29; Prov. 8:17; Matt. 7:7). When I came to the end of my rope and finally confessed to Him that there were fundamental pieces of understanding missing in my life, it was then that He faithfully opened my spiritual eyes.

In my exploration of what He meant by "know" and my disjointed revelation that solely doing for God was quite different from being with God, the puzzle worked itself forward and then backward again. It was the concept of being with God that ultimately brought to life the meaning of knowing God. That to know God and be known by God explicitly implied intimacy, unity, and oneness with Him in our lives.

Know, by biblical definition, means "to be intimately familiar with." The Merriam-Webster online dictionary goes on to define it, in archaic form, as a verb meaning "to have sexual intercourse with." We can see this phrase used repeatedly throughout Scripture to note when a man and woman came together in sexual intimacy. For example, in Genesis 4:1 we read, "And Adam knew his wife, and she conceived," just as in Matthew 1:25 it is said of Joseph toward Mary, "but [he] knew her not until she had given birth to a son." The Hebrew term used is *yada*, which carries layers of understanding in interpretation but ultimately lends to a culmination of meaning that implies deep, personal intimacy.

While at first I was put off by the concept of physical, sexual intimacy relating, in some capacity, to spiritual intimacy with God, I began to understand that there must be some weight, some substance, behind the concept of knowing and being known. If to know means to be intimately familiar with, and intimate familiarity is said all throughout His Word to create oneness, then what could God be revealing to us about oneness with Him, in Spirit, through his model of human oneness in the physical sense?

Could it be that God, the great Designer of marriage, sex, and family, fashioned right-natured relational intimacy in such a way that it reveals more of His divine character to those seeking to understand His heart? Could it be that God deeply cares about how we intimately interact with others, as it directly edifies or dismantles the picture of how He interacts with us?

Layer upon layer of connection, correlation, manifestation, and transformation flooded my mind. And while the onslaught of understanding was almost blinding—like when you remove your sunglasses and suddenly can barely squint open your adjusting eyes—I was simultaneously flooded with a supernatural peace and joy.

It was as if embracing right-natured *intimacy* became a key to rightly understanding the gospel. Over the next several months, God taught me much of what true intimacy with Him meant and how His design of relational and sexual intimacy serves as a road map for the Christ-surrendered life.

* * * * *

Let's look again at those verses in Matthew:

Not everyone who says to me, "Lord, Lord," will enter the kingdom of heaven, but the one who does the will of my Father who is in heaven. On that day many will say to me, "Lord, Lord, did we not prophesy in your name, and cast out demons in your name, and do many mighty works in your name?" And then will I declare to them, "I never knew you; depart from me, you workers of lawlessness." (Matt. 7:21–23)

We know from the Scriptures that sin and lawlessness are defined by the breaking of God's laws. And the totality of God's laws is summarized by Jesus like this:

[He asked,] "Teacher, which is the great commandment in the Law?" And [Jesus] said to him, "You shall love the Lord your God with all your heart and with all your soul and with all your mind. This is the great and first commandment. And a second is like it: You shall love your neighbor as yourself. On these two commandments depend all the Law and the Prophets." (Matt. 22:36–40)

So, in understanding the essential nature of intimate oneness with God, what we see clearly is that the workers of lawlessness failed to uphold His greatest commandment, His first invitation. No matter what list of mighty works they yielded and produced, perhaps they failed to know intimate and abiding love with God Himself.

In their doing "for" God perhaps they missed *being* with God, and rejection from eternal communion with God was the grand and disastrous result of it all.

Love. Fellowship. Intimacy. I realized, in the most delightful and equally sorrowful sense, that if our ability to grasp and experience the fullness of healing, wholeness, and salvation here on earth as it will be in heaven centers around our understanding and surrender to intimacy—right-natured and dynamic intimacy with both God and with others—then He, Himself, was going to have to teach me what that looked like. Because, probably like many of you, I looked around and realized there were only a few whole, healed, vibrant, and fruitful examples of intact, intimate relationships in my life.

Relationship, Not Religion

"It's all about relationship, not religion." We make this claim often, don't we? It's one of the foundational pillars of a believer's faith. It is the profound and wonder-working privilege directly testified to when we bear witness of Christ's love to the world.

We literally advocate for the faith by attesting to the power and willingness of El-Shaddai, God Almighty, the Maker of the heavens and the earth, to personally dwell within us and transform our hearts by way of relational love.

Yet we can look around at an inconsistent, apathetic, rebellious, and often entitled body of professed believers, and it is quickly evident there are important and eternity-shifting components missing in our understanding of the Christ-surrendered, Spirit-filled life of rich relationship. We proclaim the power of intimate relationship but are communally struggling with relational brokenness, self-serving lifestyles, fractured marriages, disjointed families, superficial friendships, and heart wounds that define our lives.

How will the world ever be enticed by an offer of intimacy with the One who has made a way for them eternally when all they see are people who don't understand how to cultivate healthy, God-honoring relationships in their own lives? If we are struggling with rightly navigating intimacy with others, could we also be struggling to rightly understand the fullness of relational intimacy with God?

Conversely, if we are framing our understanding of God's nature solely by how we have encountered broken, imperfect, or self-serving intimacy with other people, we will likely misunderstand the gospel's glorious invitation and refining grace.

◦ ● ● ● ◦

Physical fruition is a manifestation of the spiritual condition. That's an important concept to embrace as we move through the pages of this book and peel through the revelation God is ready to unpack. And that's not new age, hyperspiritual, or "enlightened" gobbledygook. It is an elementary scriptural principle we must understand if we profess to commune with and worship God both in Spirit and in truth (John 4:23–24). He is a God who is Word and also Word made flesh. Who is Spirit and also man, in Christ. He first existed and spoke, and the sound of His voice crafted the world into physical form.

What occurs in the physical world we know is a manifestation of what is occurring in the spiritual world. The collision of these realms is both real and rhythmic. They are wholly intertwined layers of our existence that testify to one another. We are spiritual beings who hold physical form for our time in this life. Whatever is going on in our earthly, physical lives points to what is going on in our spiritual lives.

Nothing is as compartmentalized as we would like to rationalize. We are complex, layered creations. We must embrace and understand that reality to ever move forward in processing Spirit-revealed insight.

The beauty of that is once we understand intimacy with Him in the Spirit, we will see healing and restoration in our intimacy with other people. As we navigate healthy intimacy with others, we will find reinforcement and encouragement in the truth of His gospel-grip on our hearts. Understanding true intimacy with God helps us understand the "why" behind His perfect design of intimacy with people, and vice versa. If we can grasp one, we will grasp the other . . . and in Jesus's name I believe we will see kingdom come on earth as it is in heaven. The two greatest commandments will mutually be fulfilled, and they will testify to one another.

So for those who are tired of shallow faith, of going through the motions, of being stuck in the same cycles, and are longing to know true intimacy with God, look with me to God's model of relational intimacy—singleness, marriage, sex, and the family unit—as a frame of reference to truly coming into oneness with Christ, embracing the process of refinement by the Holy Spirit, and living out the Great Commission as we're called to do.

I want to make it explicitly clear, as we step into unpacking how our physical relationships move through layers of progression and intimacy to prophesy the gospel, that I seek to unveil how the systems and processes God has designed for us can spiritually point us to Him. He uses physical intimacy and the evolution of right-natured relationships as one means of that, which we will explore, but they are pointers only. I pray you approach these words with a clear mind and pure heart, knowing that the sole focus is Him. Purely Him. Just Him.

Anything we think we need or cannot go without, apart from an intimate relationship with Him, is an idol. And while we can look to His design for human relationships as a model for better understanding the revelation of His gospel work, thinking we can understand God fully only once we are married or have had children or exist in a perfectly healed and whole family, we are wrong. These words are just as much for single individuals as they are for those who are wed. Understanding intimacy with God through utilizing this physical parallel of marital intimacy is for all of us, no matter our present circumstance.

Wherever you are, whatever relational condition you are in, a greater degree of intimacy with God is available to you right now. If you are single, I pray you will celebrate, right where you are, the spiritual marriage you can and are intended to presently know with Christ—no matter if God has willed marriage or children for your physical life or not. Don't let marriage be an idol in your life. After all, the apostle Paul celebrates singleness for its beautiful allowance of knowing and being known by God exclusively free of distraction. By the nature of God's love, all things should be nothing to us apart from Him. So many beautiful things are from Him and reveal Him, but if we idolize these created things over our Creator, we have misplaced our worship. We are to love nothing more than we love God, so pray in advance against forming any false belief that you can know Him and be known by Him fully only if your life parallels the seasons of life processed in these pages. They are God-given pictures that can help us see Him more clearly—but He wants all of you, right now, right where you are.

As I noted before, God is intentional. Clear. Unchanging and precise. He makes Himself explicitly available. Those who seek Him, find. When we can wrap our heads around the reality that He has given us a map, a system, a design in our physical lives that can help us see how to know Him and be known by Him in our spiritual lives, we can jump feet-first into the great adventure of seeing our relationship with Him through a new lens. And we can ultimately rest in the beauty and wonder of His multidimensional design. We can and will discover the restoration of intimacy in our lives, as well as begin to identify and rectify what stands in opposition to His model. We can find healing, freedom, and power as we seek to align our lives with His will, and His ways give us new sight.

Becoming Mary

Do you really want to know and be known by God?

Do you truly *want* intimacy? To be fully known?

Because genuine intimacy does come with great cost. Even greater gain, but also cost.

In light of His invitation to discover the *more* your soul has been longing for, will you recognize and respond? Are you willing to come out of hiding? And are you willing, for even just a little while, to stop running? To set down your Styrofoam shield of "strong Christian" and let your humanity and your vulnerability be exposed for a while?

If your answer is yes, then you're probably already wondering where we even begin on the journey of learning to abide.

I found myself nervously there too, if that's of any comfort to you. It's truly incredible how even a drop of God's living water holds the power and force of a sweeping tsunami, disorienting, dismantling, and deconstructing what we thought was sure and stable in our lives.

While I was overwhelmed and overjoyed to be coming into fresh revelation, I also began to tangibly feel the opposition of the enemy, seeking to disrupt my progress and confuse my mind. My thoughts were constantly racing. The thought . . . the startling and unnerving reminder that our God is big, vast, and complex—that there is always more of Him to know, to seek, to explore, and to discover—ignited in me a fresh urgency. But, in the same breath, it was disorienting.

Intimacy is an intimidating word when you're not sure you know how to do it "right." My long-suppressed relational issues reared their heads like vicious vipers ready to strike, and the constant, nagging lies from the enemy were deafening. I didn't know how to handle the wounds and worries that were bubbling to the surface in my heart. And I didn't like it. I didn't like the tension and discomfort and conflict that persisted in my spirit.

It's not uncommon, you know. The seasons of tension and struggle in our walks.

It's what I call "the agitation."

And, speaking from experience, it's not very much fun. It's like spiritual puberty. It's necessary but disconcerting. Awesome but equally awkward.

It's God agitating the holy hormones within us, for lack of a better term. Arousing feelings and heightening senses in the unseen realm so as to spur us on toward spiritual maturity. And it brings attempts from the enemy to stunt our growth, thwart our progress, and keep us blind. But if our goal is to grow in understanding how we can cultivate intimacy with God, then, again, we can look to our natural lives as a metaphor of what is occurring in our spiritual lives.

Did you long to know, understand, and delight in intimacy when you were a prepubescent child? Or did your interest in intimate connectedness expand only as you matured and moved through and beyond the unsettling hormone shifts of adolescence? The same can be said of our progression in the faith. There comes a point, and perhaps it is upon you now, where our elementary

36

understanding of Christ, and our first simple and euphoric encounter with His great grace, must advance. Where happiness must mature into abiding joy. Where simplicity must mature into divine depth. Where a fear of pain must mature into fortitude. Into an embrace of long-suffering surrender. Where ease must mature into enduring, steadfast assuredness. Where routine must mature into real, dynamic relationship.

Unlike physical adolescence, this is not just a one-time occurrence; our whole walk is filled with growing pains and seasons of unsettling, stirring, and often disorienting waves of tension and challenge. But, if anything, we should be encouraged by this agitation—it stands to spur transformational development in us if we remain faithfully willing and allow it.

Second Corinthians 3:18 explains this concept beautifully: "And we all, with unveiled face, beholding the glory of the Lord, are being transformed into the same image from one degree of glory to another. For this comes from the Lord who is the Spirit."

Just as our faces take shape to resemble, in ever greater degree, the mature faces of our parents as we physically age, so our spiritual growth and engagement mature us further into the likeness of Christ. From one level of glory to the next, we are invited to live by the Spirit and stay in step with the Spirit (Gal. 5:25), ultimately developing more and more into God's divine nature, even when that development is uncomfortable at times.

Psalm 84:5–7 reminds us that persevering through the tension and friction and angst actually serves to strengthen us:

> Blessed are those whose strength is in you,
>   in whose heart are the highways to Zion.
> As they go through the Valley of [Weeping]
>   they make it a place of springs;
>   the early rain also covers it with pools.
> They go from strength to strength;
>   each one appears before God in Zion.

Regardless of your physical age or the extent of time you have professed faith in Christ, such agitations are inevitable. These shifts, changes, and feelings we can't quite place are the very stimuli that progress us forward. They prompt us to explore the more we know is ahead, to wrestle through the restlessness within us until we come into our own—until we come before His throne and all His majesty.

The beauty is that God promises if we humble ourselves before Him, He will lift us up (James 4:10) in recognition of our hunger, our confusion, our fatigue, and our humanity. If we draw near to Him, He will faithfully draw near to us. It is simply our responsibility to recognize our deep need for Him to cleanse our hands and purify our hearts. We are double-minded sinners (v. 8), but He is a perfect and gracious Savior, full of compassion and pardoning mercy ready to abound. He is inviting us to return to Him, to feast at His table, and to stay awhile.

In fact, Jesus informs us that there is only one thing worth being anxious or troubled about in our lives, and that is finding our way to His feet.

> Now as they went on their way, Jesus entered a village. And a woman named Martha welcomed him into her house. And she had a sister called Mary, who sat at the Lord's feet and listened to his teaching. But Martha was distracted with much serving. And she went up to him and said, "Lord, do you not care that my sister has left me to serve alone? Tell her then to help me." But the Lord answered her, "Martha, Martha, you are anxious and troubled about many things, but one thing is necessary. Mary has chosen the good portion, which will not be taken away from her." (Luke 10:38–42)

As Martha labored, Mary rested. She listened and learned from the Messiah. As Martha toiled in good labor done unto the Lord, Mary hung on His teachings and found herself in submission to His words, spiritually feasting on the Bread of Life.

While the learning curve may seem daunting, intimacy begins with our willingness to be still and know that He is God (Ps. 46:10). Isaiah 30:15 (NLT) states, "This is what the Sovereign LORD, the Holy One of Israel says: 'Only in returning to me and resting in me will you be saved. In quietness and confidence is your strength.'"

The first true step forward toward intimacy with God is a humble step back in reverence of His Majesty. To become like Mary, with a pure-hearted posture of silence at His feet. Do you notice that she did not have to defend herself in light of her sister's complaints? Nor will you have to defend yourself in light of a world's demands you continue to prioritize the *going* and the *doing*. As if your worth is found in only what you offer, rather than who you are and whom you belong to.

No, the holy words of hope that flow from the lips of Moses stand true: "The LORD will fight for you, and you have only to be silent" (Exod. 14:14). You need only to hold a posture of presence and humility at His feet. If we long to one day stand before Him in confidence and great assurance, then we would be wise to humbly receive the invitation, today, to sit before Him, to listen and receive.

At the beginning of my journey, when I slowed my wild and worrisome heart enough to be able to rest at His feet, He spoke to me while I prayed. I hope the words He whispered to me encourage you to press in and ask Him to speak to you as well.

Be still, my daughter. Settle down. Settle in. Grow roots. Deep and wide and right where you are. I sustain and I will provide. I will not leave you barren. Your land will burst forth with life. Hope in Me. Trust in Me. Listen. I am calling you, weary-eared daughter. You have nothing to prove but to honor Me. Stop chasing what's not before you. You carry forth My favor. Only I know. Stay awhile. Be with Me. The unexpected will be seen.

So, come as you are, right where you are, and sit down with me. He is longing to teach us about intimacy that has the power to change everything.

Thank You, Abba Father, for Your perfect love.

Thank You for Your kindness and Your compassion. Your grace and Your willingness to reveal more of Yourself to us. You tell us in Matthew 7:7–11, "Ask, and it will be given to you; seek, and you will find; knock, and it will be opened to you. For everyone who asks receives, and the one who seeks finds, and to the one who knocks it will be opened. Or which one of you, if his son asks him for bread, will give him a stone? Or if he asks for a fish, will give him a serpent? If you then, who are evil, know how to give good gifts to your children, how much more will your Father who is in heaven give good things to those who ask Him!"

Father, we hold fast to Your words and we turn our faces to You, asking for nothing more and nothing less than YOU. We want to understand Your Word, Father. We want to truly know You and be known by You. Please give us supernatural humility. Please give us a great measure of patience. Please give us eyes to see and ears to hear as we search Your Word and seek Your face. God, I pray the blood of Yeshua over these pages, and I pray for an outpouring of understanding and sight. Lord, grant me understanding, healing, faith, hope, and permission to wrestle through the tensions in my heart. Where the Spirit of the Lord is, there is freedom. I pray You would breathe life and freedom into every page moving forward.

Amen.

our intended identity

No matter who we are, where we are, or what season of life we physically find ourselves in, the understanding of true spiritual intimacy with God begins in the same place for every one of us: the garden. Rightly understanding where things began and who we were created to be not only serves to restore our broken perception of God's character but also serves to restore our broken perception of ourselves. And those two things are of paramount importance. *If we want to know intimacy, we must first know our identity.* Just like the healthiest physical relationships unfold when both parties are individually confident in who they are and are able to celebrate stable trust in one another, so spiritual intimacy is built upon a solid foundation of trust and an assurance of our worth.

For many, the word *intimacy* and the thought of intimately communing with God feels perverted, abusive, inaccessible, awkward, or unobtainable. It is a strange concept to grab hold of, not because it is strange in and of itself (in fact, it is a biblically foundational concept) but because all we have ever really known is a long-term and volatile relationship with lies. We have been communing with the deceiver, the enemy who is on a mission to steal, kill, and destroy any hope of a healthy relationship with the One we were made to know—the One we were designed by and created to know perfect oneness with. And, as a result, the concept of intimacy with a spiritual being mighty enough to craft the heavens and the earth feels like a completely flighty and foreign concept. Even for those who have professed faith for years of their lives.

But the truth is that we physically exist in a fallen, sinful world that Satan is presently ruling over (John 12:31). God Himself is the sovereign Author and Authority over all of creation, and we know from the first chapter of the book of Job that the enemy can only carry out what God has given permission for. But we can also see that the overall mission of the deceiver, while he has any time left before he is cast into the lake of fire, is to drag down with him as many of God's created beings as possible. This fallen world, and all of the spiritual rulers, powers, world forces of darkness, and forces of evil in the spiritual realm (Eph. 6:12) have been systematically deceiving and desensitizing us to believe countless inaccurate and disjointed ideas about God and about ourselves. And that has spilled over into so many of our physical relationships and interactions as well. In order for our minds to be truly renewed, we have to open ourselves to the idea that things are not as surface-level and one-dimensional as they seem.

For example, with regard to God's character, if you are anything like me, I would imagine your primary perceptions of Him are heavily reflective of the character traits of your earthly father or various other authority figures or even people you have been physically involved with who have woven their way through your life so far. Imperfect people influencing our core beliefs about a perfect heavenly Father is very problematic. And, equally, a very real layer of influence we all must navigate through.

As a result, you may perceive God as inaccessible, abusive, volatile, or apt to abandon you. You may perceive Him as apathetic or disengaged, manipulative or unpredictable. Crude or a liar or ultimately disgusted with you. Annoyed with the complex layers of your humanity and likely tapped out on extending you any further compassion or grace. You've likely reinforced your own confused thoughts by skimming the Word of God and misinterpreting or misunderstanding elements of Scripture passages you've hastily bitten off without digesting the full feast of His Word. Maybe you believe He is just tolerating you, is eager to condemn you, or is ultimately unconcerned with the days of your life or the state of your eternity because you're just *too much*—too much of any number of disqualifying things.

Because the *you* whom you think God perceives takes any number of shapes and forms based on your circumstances, emotions, fears, or insecurities, you may ultimately feel like a filthy, worthless, weak failure. An inconvenience, a burden, or a nuisance. Or perhaps you bounce back and forth between believing you are inconsequential, a cluster of cells whose life is ultimately meaningless, to then feeling as though the weight of the world rests on your shoulders or that you are the god of your own life. You fluctuate between purposelessness and pride, fear and self-sufficiency. But, nevertheless, you remain crushed by the heavy burden of your imperfect attempts to control what's around you and the paralyzing fear that God doesn't even pay mind to you. Maybe you have even been preached at from this angle: that you are fundamentally an inconsequential, hopeless being, and thank goodness that an inaccessible, angry God took pity on you.

Or maybe you don't feel any of these extremes. Perhaps when it comes to your thoughts about God's nature and about whom He made you to be, you are relatively disengaged, stoic, or shallow in your investment in the "relationship" you claim. What an equally disturbing point of view.

But the reality is that even in light of all these formative misperceptions, God still earnestly longs to reveal to you *what is true*. To reconstruct the foundations of your understanding. To expose truth that invites right-natured intimacy to be the rhythm of your story. When I was crying out in my baby's bedroom, longing to know why I felt so far from the Father I wanted so badly to please, I realized I perceived my heavenly Father to be just like my earthly dad, and I was pandering for His approval through my performance.

If you've read my first book, *Wreck My Life*, you may remember my struggles with perfectionism and the agonizing pain and rejection I suffered when the daddy whose approval I longed for ended his own life. Those unhealthy efforts to perform for approval were very evident in my life before I came to know Christ, but I thought I was beyond those wounds. When I realized, many years into my journey with the Lord, that they were still dictating the strides of my walk of faith, I was disoriented. However, as God began revealing to me that His character was quite different than the only fatherly frame of reference I held, He did not chastise me or shame me for my ignorance and blind spots; He simply reminded me of my identity. He spoke gentle words of encouragement to my soul. And lifted me up to stand firm on my feet, reminding me that Christ's work on the cross was sufficient. By His blood I was, in fact, still a daughter of the Most High King. And that revelation—that truth so gently washed back over me—was the catalyst that changed everything.

You see, the good news of the gospel is ultimately that there is a way, a hope, and a truth we can come alive to and believe in that, by His great grace, speaks our true identity over us, transforms us, and rescues us from the lies we've been abused by for far too long. But, while it's certainly important to tackle and dismantle the lies, the wounds, and the actions that have manifested as evidence of deception in our lives, the enemy doesn't get the privilege in these pages of being acknowledged first. No, the place of primary attention and blessing goes to the goodness and the glory of the One True God. The Holy One of Israel. In fact, most of these pages will be devoted to revealing who He truly is, because His character qualities and His nature come to life in vibrant and fresh ways through every step of the intimate, uniting process of living in gospel rhythm. After all, Romans 2:4 reminds us that it is the kindness of God that leads us to repentance—the turning away from sin and turning toward God. It is the love and kindness of God that compels our hearts to turn back to Him and His truth.

But to say we, in recognition of our sin, turn *back* in repentance is to imply that we are not where we once were. We are not where we are intended to be. And there is a holy invitation to return. A turning back toward what was first created as *good* in the eyes of the Lord and what was intended in the beginning.

So, in order to truly understand intimacy with God, we begin by understanding our intended identity. We begin in the same place His Word knows genesis—the garden. Creation. Where God reveals Himself as supreme and reveals to us the full image of who we are intended to be, whose we are intended to be, and whom we are being invited to come back to in order to encounter the true intimacy our souls long for, both now and for eternity.

As It Was Intended to Be

We were made by God in His image. With intentionality. And purpose. And specific, divine detail. We were fashioned to reflect His likeness, His character, and His nature. The Maker of the heavens and earth, the most supreme eternal Authority, made both you and me to bear and reflect what He is like to the physical world.

> Then God said, "Let us make man in our image, after our likeness. And let them have dominion over the fish of the sea and over the birds of the heavens and over the livestock and over all the earth and over every creeping thing that creeps on the earth." So God created man in his own image, in the image of God he created him; male and female he created them. (Gen. 1:26–27)

The Hebrew word translated here as "man," *adam*, is the generic term for humankind. This is why the passage goes on to use

45

the plural pronoun "them." So, in this context we see that God is speaking of both men and women. Both are made in the likeness of God—unique and distinctly different—and both carry important and divine characteristics of God in their very design.

Man and woman, equal in dignity, value, importance, and worth, both powerfully reflect incredible elements of His likeness. We see equal and dynamic reflections of God's nature complement one another to display His beautiful character. And, ultimately, through the original design of man and woman, He intended that we see a tangible, physical picture of who He is, how He spiritually exercises dominion over creation, and how He creates life.

We talked before about how we are both spiritual and physical beings. For context, we see this displayed in Yeshua—Jesus Christ is both the Son of God and the Son of Man (Rom. 1:3–4). The Word of God in perfect inhabitation of human flesh (John 1:14), the visible image of the invisible God, for in Him all the fullness of God dwelled (Col. 1:15–20). So, yes, Jesus Christ was and is fully God and fully man—the Son of God inhabiting the physical, fleshed frame of a man among us.

It's important we also realize that though we are not Christ, of course—He, alone, is the head of the body—humans were not created to be one-dimensional, inconsequential, barren dust. We are not just physical cells. Not just natural beings—arms and legs and eyes and brains that are wasting away. No, Genesis 2:7 (NLT) says, "The LORD God formed the man from the dust of the ground" (the physical) then continues, "He breathed the breath of life into the man's nostrils, and the man became a living person" (the spiritual). God, a spiritual being, breathed out His divine breath at creation, and the mysterious and miraculous measure of God birthed a spiritual being who was created as His offspring (Acts 17:29).

What's more, He then noted, as the man was carrying out the task of care and dominion over what God the Father had given him to steward, that it was not good that man should be alone. And the Creator resolved to make a helper fit for him (Gen. 2:18).

So the LORD God caused a deep sleep to fall upon the man, and while he slept took one of his ribs and closed up its place with flesh. And the rib that the LORD God had taken from the man he made into a woman and brought her to the man.

Then the man said,

> "This at last is bone of my bones
>   and flesh of my flesh;
> she shall be called Woman,
>   because she was taken out of man." (vv. 21–23)

I believe God drew woman from man so that the fullness of His character and nature could be realized. That, in tandem, they form a dynamic and complementary picture of who He is, as both leader and helper, authority and colaborer, guide and support, justice and mercy, reverent fear and nurturing love, so God could be known and cultivated and reflected to the world in the balanced relationship of man and woman.

Our design, our makeup, our inherent anatomy as male or female, made intentionally by God, stamps miraculous worth over us. Our form and function bear powerful and specific witness to God's nature and likeness. And, not only that, the intentionality exercised as He made humankind in the garden shows the careful and powerful attention to divine detail God wove together in you.

Do you understand what this means at the most basic level? God was perfectly intentional as He formed this physical display of the spiritual realm. He perfectly planned how and why and who He created. And that's just page 6 of my Bible! Genesis 1:31 begins by saying, "And God saw everything he had made, and behold, it was very good" (NLT). Your life is valuable—made by a Maker. Behold, you're worth knowing and being known. His handiwork in you—it is very good.

You are not an accident or unimportant. You were delightfully designed. Humankind was originally formed, at creation, as offspring, children . . . spiritual family members of God Almighty.

What a beautiful Father He is! What a joy it must have been for the Maker to bring into visibility His miraculous design of humankind. The physical reflections of His spiritual nature, offspring of a heavenly Father invited to know Him, worship Him, and delight in His creation. We were first deemed sons and daughters of the Most High God. Can you comprehend the power of our intended identity?

Rightly understanding our identity at creation not only helps restore our broken perception of our worth—who we were made to be and who we are restored as, through Christ—but also helps us rightly see the Creator. The One who formed and fashioned us and gifted us with all that was good. And when we look to the garden, we see one of the primary purposes for which we were formed by Him: to commune with Him. To know perfect unity with Him. To exist in intimate relationship and oneness with God Himself. How great our Maker is!

So why, then? Why did he make us man and woman? Why does it matter so deeply that we know who He says we are? Why is intimacy with Him so much more powerfully cultivated when we see the fullness of His handiwork in the beginning?

Because not only did He make us in great delight, He made us with gospel story–telling intent woven into our design. Humankind was formed as not just a dynamic reflection of Himself but also a dynamic expression of His gospel plan. Because He was intent on saving us even before we knew we would need saving. Nothing that was, is, or is to come is ever out of His sight, plan, or grasp. Every detail of His Word from page 1 is woven together to wrap you up and draw you to His heart. Back to the garden. Back to your true spiritual identity in and through Him.

The whole of His Word speaks in layers. So, while the first chapters of Genesis are very much a physical account of His creation, they are simultaneously (like the entirety of the Word) a prophetic picture breathed out to help us understand the spiritual realm. To help us understand God.

To understand more clearly what I'm saying, let's look first at the first man, Adam. And let's pray to spiritually see the symbolism woven through God's Word. Remember Adam's formation from the *dust?* Genesis 2:4–5 notes that the dust was barren and lifeless because the Lord Himself had not yet sent the rain to water the earth. The dust is representative of our bodies, our physical form. Barren and lifeless, ultimately, apart from Him. But God Himself sent springs to water the land (v. 6), just as He sent Christ, the Living Water, so that our flesh may be saturated by His grace. Then He breathed the *breath of life* into Adam, and he became a living person. The breath represents the Holy Spirit—the power of God.

Dust represents the created man. Water represents Christ. And breath represents the Spirit of God. Adam became a living person. Dust, water, and breath resulted in physical life just as the created man, Christ, and the power of the Holy Spirit result in our spiritual life! We were never intended to just be flesh here, not insignificant, not just a cluster of cells. No, that is a lifeless misunderstanding of self and a belief that will lead to eternal death. We were formed by the Father to drink of the Living Water of Christ and to be resuscitated by the very breath of God that we may be spiritually living people, both now and for eternity, who are no longer barren but can bear fruit!

The formation of humankind even portrays the gospel. And, knowing God took physical form as the Son of Man, in Christ, we can also understand *man* as a prophetic reflection of *Jesus*. The Bridegroom. The husband. So, when we look at God's design of marriage, the man, the husband—all are a physical picture given to us to understand the position of Christ in our lives and hearts. As authority and leader. As lover and groom. As provider and disciplinarian. As protector and our covering. As the head. His powerful and absolute yet honorable and inviting leadership is intended to be displayed through the male figure.

And then there is *woman*, remember, removed from man's side? She so magnificently represents the church—the people of God, always intended to know themselves as bone of Christ's bone, flesh of His flesh—offspring of God, members of His spiritual family. You see, in Genesis 2:18, when God reflected that it was not good for man to be alone, He reveals to us His heart for intimacy and family. He longed for multiplication, that Christ would be the firstborn from the dead, the firstborn among many brethren. The Creator made woman to complement man, as man alone did not reflect the fullness of God's nature in dominion over creation. Just as woman was made from man, so the *ecclesia* (the church, the people called out from the world for God) was made from Christ! Out of Adam's rib came Eve, just as Christ was pierced under his rib on the cross and blood and water flowed out. In his death on the cross, the church was taken out from Him—covered in His blood and saturated in Living Water, that the world may see a beautiful and full reflection of God's nature through those who follow Him and humbly colabor in service with Him.

In the formation of woman, we can see a picture of God's full plan of the formation and multiplication of His church. His offspring. His bride. When we look at God's design for marriage, the woman, the wife—all are a physical picture given to us to understand the position and role all believers carry (male and female alike) in the full story of God. As helper and colaborer. As lover and bride. As nurturer and caretaker of His family. As those living in trust, submission, humility, obedience, service, and delight. Strong and fierce and resilient; powerful, complex, dynamic, smart, and gifted. All the dynamic and vibrant traits that make up a woman are expressions of all He intended His people, His church, to be.

Ephesians 5:31–33 reinforces this parallel of man and woman when it says,

> "Therefore a man shall leave his father and mother and hold fast to his wife, and the two shall become one flesh." This mystery is profound, and I am saying that it refers to Christ and the church.

However, let each one of you love his wife as himself, and let the wife see that she respects her husband.

The wonder of His detail! Just scratching the surface reveals perfect intentionality by the Maker—and reminds us of the identity always offered us. The great value of our lives.

Seeing the Gospel through the Sexual Design

Man and woman. Christ and the church. The Bridegroom and the bride. As I explored more of His true nature and my identity in Him, God consistently pointed me toward the parallels between each pairing and the natural progression of how healthy relationship was supposed to play out within these covenantal unions. Sexual intimacy is most certainly an undeniable relational component between a bridegroom (man) and a bride (woman), so what significance could it carry in relationship to Christ and His church? How did the pieces connect?

As I was reading His Word one day, God dropped a "key" into my spirit in the form of a single word: *oneness.*

Adam and Eve were one with God in the garden, before sin entered in and caused division. Because they knew holy oneness with Him, they could stand naked and unashamed before Him. The ultimate purpose of the cross, the power of Christ's blood, is to atone for sin and make a way for us to return to His presence. To know oneness with God again. Ultimately returning to a place of standing spiritually naked and unashamed before God, united and fully known.

Think about it this way: if man equates to Christ and woman equates to His followers, then ultimately, we all—men and women alike—can see and understand ourselves through the lens of *bride.* Wife. As well as through the lens of all the women who appear in Scripture. Now apply that understanding to this passage: "This explains why a man leaves his father and mother and is joined to his

51

wife, and the two are united into one. Now the man and his wife were both naked, but they felt no shame" (Gen. 2:24–25 NLT).

Why did Christ leave the heavenly, spiritual realm, as well as His heavenly Father? Our Bridegroom, in the very public act of the cross, proposed for us a *union*. And when we, in light of His great grace, choose to receive that sacrificial act with faith, we become His bride and are joined to Him. A husband and wife come together in physical intimacy, to "know" each other and to become "one," and as Christ's bride we are invited into oneness with Him on a spiritual level. Through our dynamic, active, and intimate relationship with Him, we will one day be perfectly unified. Progressively purified by His great love. Transformed by His patience and mercy. Disarmed by His great compassion and grace. And, ultimately, healed, emboldened, and restored to our place of birthright—the garden. The place of holy oneness with the One who made us and made a way for us to come home.

Yes, at creation, things were as they were intended to be. Man and woman were made with great intention, and they knew perfect oneness with God. The garden was a place of flawless intimacy and communion. A place where miraculous humankind was fully known and fully knew the voice, the guidance, the love, and the blessing of the Father. Where we stood before Him and before one another, fully exposed, bare, and seen. Our hearts nude and known. We had direct access to God, and God's intent for His children—to live obedient, purpose-filled, honoring lives—was perfectly cultivated in holiness, completely separated from evil.

The invitation of the gospel is to return to that place of relational oneness by faith. We were made for it.

Perfect, dynamic, full, revealing, abiding intimacy with God. Intimacy that is holy, unblemished, dynamic, and sure. Intimacy that bears good fruit!

It's hard to fully understand how we could possibly know God in that way. But just as a newlywed couple may think they know all about love and are blissfully unified, the truth is that a seasoned couple who has navigated marriage for decades has much to teach them about the fullness of what it means to know each other and be one. The journey, the challenges, the learning curves, the work required. All are gained from commitment to the covenant and pursuit of one another's hearts over time. Similarly, though we may like to think that at the moment of entering into relationship with Jesus we immediately understand what spiritual intimacy is, the truth is there is always more of God's heart to explore, seasons to journey through, and layer upon layer of ourselves to relinquish to His refining love.

I believe that's one reason the gift of right-natured physical intimacy (within the right context) was given to humankind. It is an image given to help us understand, perceive, and better understand God's spiritual design of *yada*.

All of creation is made and meant to reflect the image and heart of God (Ps. 8:1; 19:1; John 1:3). Every system, every process, every detail points us back to Him. Everything we can tangibly touch, see, and experience. For those with faith to believe in what is unseen, He gives eyes to understand how what we can see and touch and taste and feel ultimately tell the story of who He is and how we are intended to experience Him spiritually.

> For since the creation of the world God's invisible qualities—his eternal power and divine nature—have been clearly seen, being understood from what has been made, so that people are without excuse. (Rom. 1:20 NIV)

This is also why, in Luke 19:40, Jesus tells the Pharisees that even if the disciples stopped proclaiming His name and His glory, the very stones would cry out! Because the whole earth is full of His glory (Isa. 6:3). He is organized and orderly and misses no detail. All His creation shows us Himself, His glorious gospel plan, and His invitation back to unity with Him. Every element and facet of His creation reveals to us His nature. And this includes the gift of physical intimacy He gave us, as man and woman. He uses all His design to speak to His people. Everything and all things exist to draw us back to the intimacy we long to know and remind us of His will for our lives.

To know Him. To be known by Him. *Truly.*

It's the deep and growling hunger in our starving souls. And it begins, powerfully, by seeing His goodness and His divine detail in His creation of humankind. We are not to worship the created thing—not man nor woman nor marriage nor sex—but rather the Creator! We can always find more of Him in and through His creations, ultimately. He has been so good to us and fashioned us in His love from the beginning of time. The Maker longs for those He made to turn their hearts back to Him. He longs to deconstruct the weak foundation of lies we have built shaky houses upon, and He is inviting His family to return home. Step-by-step. One layer of understanding at a time.

● ● ◗ ◖ ●

So, after the agitation of spiritual puberty and the recognition of our God-breathed identity, where are we on the journey of maturing intimacy? Where the gospel meets us all: in our state of spiritual "singleness." And in some of the messy and confusing repercussions that take shape in our physical lives as well as our spiritual lives when sin dangles the bait of spiritual autonomy.

Our heavenly Father always intended for humankind to live holy lives free from evil, because He Himself is perfectly holy. And thus darkness cannot exist in His presence. As 1 John 1:5 shows us, the Father is perfect. He is light, and in Him there is no darkness at all. Evil and holiness cannot coexist. But, in the same breath, true love cannot exist without the free will of choice. Intimate love is never an act of force; therefore, in His perfect lovingkindness, He shows us *all* of the divine and miraculous layers at hand, but He also planted *choice* in the garden. One of the most intimate acts of true love.

What we see, though, in both the garden as well as in the full story of our humanity, is that our present flesh is weak (Matt. 26:41). And despite having the free will to choose the right-natured intimacy God always intended, both spiritually and physically, we are prone to wander. We are easily deceived. And with choice planted before us, we first chose, and often continue to choose, wrongly.

Heavenly Father,

You are unfathomable! Your design, Your Word, Your ways—incomprehensible! Thank You so much, Father, for forming and fashioning man and woman—for forming and fashioning me! Thank You so much for life—for the very breath in my lungs—and for the inherent value You knit into Your creation. Father, please help me understand. Please give me vision of the garden; give me vision of perfect, holy oneness with You. Give me revelation of Your goodness, Your love, Your power, and Your kindness now, so when I feel weary, tired, confused, and worthless, Your Spirit can testify to mine—reminding me who my Maker is! Give me revelation of Your truth, shown to us in the garden, so when temptation overwhelms me, or sin threatens me with an unyielding grip, it is of no burden to claim the blood of Your Son Jesus over it, to throw it off, to flee, to repent and return to where I was made to belong. Back to You . . . back to Your heart. I thank You so much for Your voice—that You are always speaking. That You are, in so many ways, the best kind of mystery to seek and to find. I long to stand naked and unashamed before You spiritually, God. There is so much within me that inhibits that—so much lingering sin, so many wounds, so much pain and fear that force me to, like Eve, hide behind fig leaves. But I have faith to believe that Your love is sufficient. Your mercy is sufficient.

Your grace is sufficient to shine light into the darkness and welcome me out of hiding, step-by-step on this journey. Thank You for Your patience, God. You are so good. You are worthy of all praise.

Amen.

spiritual "singleness"

The gift of choice—of free will—rests at the very core of true love, of true intimacy. To stay or to go, to obey or disobey, to abide or abandon. These are the choices before us in God's design of relational intimacy. The freedom to go or disobey or abandon is the very thing that makes the choice to stay and obey and abide all the more valuable. True intimacy does not come by force, manipulation, or imprisonment. True intimacy is fostered where freedom is found. And, with freedom, the choice to stay and submit and commune becomes the soil from which beautiful fruit abounds.

God is safe. And sure. And a promise keeper. He also loves His creations. So much so that He planted choice at the center of our hearts. In the center of the garden.

Genesis 2:8–10 describes,

> Then the Lord God planted a garden in Eden in the east, and there he placed the man he had made. The Lord God made all sorts of trees grow up from the ground—trees that were beautiful and that produced delicious fruit. In the middle of the garden he placed the tree of life and the tree of the knowledge of good and evil. A

river flowed from the land of Eden, watering the garden and then dividing into four branches. (NLT)

At the center of Eden, with living water branching into four parts, and at the center of our four-chambered heart, God planted choice. The tree of life, which held eternal promise, and the tree of the knowledge of good and evil, which ultimately held death in choosing its enticing fruit. This is what was set before humankind, and this is where one clear instruction was given.

> The LORD God took the man and put him in the garden of Eden to work it and keep it. And the LORD God commanded the man, saying, "You may surely eat of every tree of the garden, but of the tree of the knowledge of good and evil you shall not eat, for in the day that you eat of it you shall surely die." (Gen. 2:15–17)

You see, God not only loves us enough to give us choice but also loves us so much that He gives us guidance and instruction for our good. In right-natured intimacy and communion with Him, we are not left blind but rather He gives us His Word of Life. For our good. For our protection. It was, initially, just one instruction given. Just one law: choose God. Obey Him. He loves us and offers us everything we need, everything that will truly satisfy our soul and give us purpose and joy and eternal life.

But with freedom, in light of choice, and faced with temptation from the deceiver, the flesh proved weak. The mind and heart of humankind was easily deceived. And what we see in the garden in Genesis 3:1–7 is that Satan set out on a mission, primed and focused, to separate humankind from God, to break up the Father from His children, to fracture holy unity, oneness, and family. He enticed Eve to disobey, to break God's one law, with an invitation to be her own god on her own terms. This invitation to false freedom—what a grip it has on us. And in choosing to commune with the deceiver and follow him, humankind broke God's one law and sin entered into the garden (1 John 3:4), into God's holy marriage bed, and spiritual death became our portion (Rom. 6:23). Not because God desired that for humankind but because we chose it. And because, ruled by our flesh, we continue to choose it every day. The sin of pride, the very thing that caused Lucifer's fall, was the STD, the spiritually transmitted disease, that infected the body of humankind when we disobeyed.

Pride, in my opinion, rests at the core of all of our sin.

Though created for holy intimacy and communion, we became unholy. The human heart chose spiritual adultery from our One True Love, and now passes down the filthy infection from generation to generation in our fallen flesh. God honored our choice by giving us over to the perversion we preferred (Rom. 1:24); again, true intimacy is never cultivated by force but rather choice. And we chose separation. We chose, and often continue to choose, our own desires because they are falsely disguised as freedom, an offer of "singleness." We desire autonomy and take the bait, but we fail to realize we are actually being trafficked, enslaved by sin. We leave our Father's house to live in the brothel of a fallen world presently governed by an abuser.

Just like Esau foolishly gave up his birthright and inheritance to Jacob in exchange for one meal—one momentary urge and desire of his flesh—in Genesis 25 (and reiterated in Heb. 12:16), so humankind forfeited and squandered our inheritance for the momentary temptation of prideful lust. And today, in our flesh, we remain predisposed to do the same.

First John 5:19 tells us the whole world presently lies in the power of the evil one. And 2 Corinthians 4:3 confirms this when Paul says the god of this fallen world has blinded the minds of the unbelievers. Revelation 12:9 reveals this truth and exposes the goal of Satan and his fallen angels: to deceive the entire world in the time they have before God's final justice comes. The devil's aim from the beginning was to entice the whole world to spiritual adultery, to lust after and put anything—any want, any urge, any desire, any idol—above the One who has never been and would never be unfaithful. The One whose love is perfect, and whose intimate presence conceives in us the fullness of truth, power, love, and eternal life.

But sin seduces us into a sickbed and into consequences and suffering. We see this throughout His Word—the bride of Christ in contrast to the great prostitute (Rev. 17). Sin entices us to forsake our first true love (Rev 2:4), and Rev. 2:19–23 goes on to illustrate this truth:

> I know your works, your love and faith and service and patient endurance, and that your latter works exceed the first. But I have this against you, that you tolerate that woman Jezebel, who calls herself a prophetess and is teaching and seducing my servants to practice sexual immorality and to eat food sacrificed to idols. I gave her time to repent, but she refuses to repent of her sexual immorality. Behold, I will throw her onto a sickbed, and those who commit adultery with her I will throw into great tribulation, unless they repent of her works, and I will strike her children dead. And all the churches will know that I am he who searches mind and heart, and I will give to each of you according to your works.

We asked for a separation in the garden and opted for what we perceived to be the better route—autonomy, void of commitment, in hopes it would satisfy and live up to the allure it offered. But, as I personally learned so many times in the hardest ways through my own testimony of sexual brokenness, in sin we are always choosing friendship with a shallow world rather than true and transformational intimacy with God. And the greatest sorrow is that our blindness to that reality only continues to deceive us about who God really is and what pure intimacy with Him is intended to look like. When we came out from under the protection and authority of our Father and, like the prodigal son, rebelled and left our Father's house, our hearts were steered into what I like to call "the brothel." And, in rejecting spiritual life and instead choosing to be lorded by our dying flesh, we find our spiritual "singleness" has fostered in humanity an unquenchable hunger for acceptance and connection, as well as an enslavement to every counterfeit, ungodly offer of wholeness. That spiritual condition manifests in innumerable physical conditions that grip us individually and culturally. But these physical symptoms all point back to spiritual sickness and can help us understand the true root of infection as they testify to one another.

I want to encourage you that the chapters to come are chock-full of truth, edification, equipment, and applicable "hows" to walking in holy and right-natured intimacy. But the sight—the revelation of the roots behind some of our most dynamic challenges and seemingly shameful shackles—can be really hard to confront. Receiving this depth of revelation from the Spirit was truly heavy for me—namely because I have wrestled through almost every issue on the list in some shape or form. But I pray you'll join me in persevering. While I found the revelation convicting and hard to receive, it ultimately served to break chains off of my life and my marriage and to bring greater freedom into my story. Seeing how I was being deceived spiritually . . . seeing some of my actions and choices through the eyes and heart of God and letting that magnification marinate in my heart—well, it ultimately deeply refined me. And drew me to a place of even purer intimacy with God that I would not trade for anything. I pray this revelatory sight serves you in the same way.

The pages of this book couldn't begin to hold the full number of physical examples that grant us insight into spiritual issues that ultimately serve to deceive us about the truth of God's heart and what intimacy with Him is intended to look like. But in my grief and in repentance of my own heart issues, the Lord opened my eyes to the spiritual conditions behind a handful of common physical things in our world—and even in His body of professed believers—that grieve Him. These things stand in antithesis to His design and keep our minds blinded and confused to His true nature. They are areas of disobedience and darkness that cause disconnection from God and keep us imprisoned spiritually. And I want to shine light on them not to shame you but to expose darkness for what it is and invite you into the freedom we were always intended to walk in. God takes no pleasure in the spiritual death of anyone, so if you find that one of these conditions exists in your life, or if you have been afflicted with the evil of one of these areas of brokenness, I pray you will turn back to Him to know true life (Ezek. 18:30–32). His grace is sufficient, every single time we call upon Him with an earnest heart.

1. Self-Love

Masturbatory is an adjective defined as "excessively self-absorbed or self-indulgent." And "masturbatory faith" was the very phrase God spoke to my spirit one afternoon as I prayed and sought His heart concerning the primary source of powerlessness and purposelessness rampant in the body of Christ. While you may initially rear up at the mention of both masturbation and faith in the same sentence, the truth is that they are wholly intertwined and testify to self-worship and a lack of self-control in both the physical and spiritual sense. I'm often asked if I believe masturbation is a sin, because the Word of God does not directly spell it out in plain text. Or does it? The physical acts we indulge in ultimately reveal if we are ruled by our flesh or by the Spirit—are we "excessively self-absorbed or self-indulgent"?

> But understand this, that in the last days there will come times of difficulty. For people will be *lovers of self*, lovers of money, proud, arrogant, abusive, disobedient to their parents, ungrateful, unholy, heartless, unappeasable, slanderous, *without self-control*,

brutal, not loving good, treacherous, reckless, swollen with conceit, *lovers of pleasure rather than lovers of God*, having the appearance of godliness, but denying its power. Avoid such people. For among them are those who creep into households and capture weak women, *burdened with sins and led astray by various passions, always learning and never able to arrive at a knowledge of the truth.* (2 Tim. 3:1–7, emphasis mine)

I find that most everyone who musters the courage to ask me about masturbation is carrying a heavy burden they can't quite put their finger on. I know that was the case in my life when I struggled with masturbation. When conviction is present yet stuffed down, we aren't able to understand the truth: when we give in to every craving and desire and urge of our body, we are ultimately living chained to our depraved state. Ultimately revealing we still live in the brothel of our flesh. Galatians 5:19–21 makes it clear that the deeds of the flesh are evident and include impurity, sensuality, and idolatry, and those who practice these things will not inherit the kingdom of heaven. Romans 13:14 encourages us to make no provision for the flesh in regard to its lusts and Ephesians 2:3 makes it clear that when we indulge the desires of the flesh and of the mind we're still, by nature, children of wrath.

One of the main elements of idolatry here is that masturbation puts another god before the One True King, and that god is yourself. You serve your wants, your own urges, your own body when your flesh demands it, rather than yielding to the Spirit in self-control (Gal. 5:22–23). You worship yourself. This physical act reflects the spiritual reality that you put yourself above God, and self-focused faith is the rotten fruit that hangs from such ragged vines.

When I saw spiritual evidence of this in my life and had to earnestly repent, I realized I was solely chasing the "highs" of God. The mountaintop experiences and surges. We want what we want, when we want it, as soon as we want it, and by our own hand. We do not desire spiritual accountability. We do not want to invest in the work, surrender, diligence, and transparency necessary for a true marriage to our Bridegroom. We want a compulsive result empty of thought, pursuit, investment, and sacrifice. We desire a God who will meet our instantaneous wants more than we desire to know and be known by the One True God who is both present and promised.

We approach the throne of grace in a self-serving, self-seeking posture that ultimately demands the immediacy of God's blessing, answer, or power in exactly the way we desire. We are not familiar with long-enduring intimacy but rather live lorded by the lure of the instantaneous emotional rush. We want to be the one with the microphone, the expert on all matters, the one teaching and leading in any area we choose. We want to be the influencer. We lust after the platforms, longing to be elevated for our own name's sake at our own speedy pace—spiritual narcissism is the posture of our hearts. We don't want to be known by God; we just want the benefits of God. And that is a "walk of faith" that is hell-bound, not holy.

When the high fades and the daily rhythm of walking yielded to Him in obedience and trust is required, we don't know how to cultivate longevity. When God does not move at the pace or speed we believe is best, we doubt Him and reject Him and, foolishly, seek to determine our life on our own terms. We do not live by the Spirit or stay in step with the Spirit as Galatians 5:25 advises.

Masturbatory faith is a fake faith, just like physical masturbation is a fake intimacy. A life and heart lorded by the flesh. And it ultimately deceives us into believing God is only good when things feel good in life. This is a deep-rooted lie that hinders us from truly knowing the fullness of His nature.

2. Spiritual Porn

Watching porn, viewing explicit images, fantasizing, and bringing porn into the bedroom falls into a similar camp of spiritual perversion and deception. Physical intimacy is sacred and holy, an act of worship between a husband and wife. It is intended for intimate connection and oneness, removed from the world, undistracted. It is the most unifying entangler of souls, reflects the gospel powerfully (as we'll unpack in the coming chapters), and bears beautiful physical fruit. But porn is a counterfeit copy of this act that is staged, defiling, often physically and verbally violent, and a cheap imitation that drips with lewd and animalistic carnality. All packaged and edited for our viewing pleasure, complete with production value and shiny façades that invite us into experience (seemingly free of consequence) what our flesh is longing to feel and see.

When we are tempted to watch porn for entertainment and arousal, we are feeding off the rush of viewing an act that God designed to be intimate and hidden. We are sitting in on something we inherently know we should not see, ultimately committing adultery by Scripture's standards (Matt. 5:28) and allowing our mind and physical body to experience counterfeit arousal—though we are momentarily convinced the rush experienced is a good-enough version of the real thing. It looks like the real thing but it is not. It makes us believe we've experienced the real thing but actually leaves us dead and alone, with no other life around us.

This deeply perverts our understanding of true intimacy with God, because not only is our perception of intimate exchange seen through a perverted, evil, and lascivious lens but we also begin to retire to spiritual viewership, convinced that solely looking upon someone else's spiritual intimacy through their revelation and teaching and packaged presentation is a good-enough version of the real thing. While there is certainly nothing wrong with others sharing revelations, teaching, and building the body with their words, if we are not careful we can find ourselves in a consumptive posture so fixated on observing the Spirit move through others that we completely neglect engaging with the Spirit of God ourselves.

Watching compelling clips on our favorite pastor's Instagram feed is not synonymous with spending intimate time with God ourselves. Consuming videos, podcasts, and recorded messages from our favorite leaders in the faith is not synonymous with spending time in prayer and praise before His throne. Just as pornography consumption has been rising in startling quantities in recent years, I also see a rising tide of consumptive Christianity in our nation. Convenient viewing of other people's relationships with God has disguised itself as sufficient and left many disconnected from engaging with the Spirit personally.

We chase the big conferences and the flashy speakers and the expensive invitations to worship God alongside bestselling recording artists, convinced we may encounter something better and more pleasurable through that viewing platform than we could in our own prayer closet, communing in the Spirit with Christ. We often feast on the words of other imperfect people who have a high follower count on social media more readily than we digest the Word of God for ourselves. We are often drawn to things that look alive while we are actually dead. We gravitate toward displays of intimacy with God but struggle with true intimacy ourselves. And ultimately, we isolate ourselves from truly relating with God or with others; we settle for the surge of what we feel while watching from a distance without engaging with God. But this is not God's desire for our lives.

God wants to know you and be known by you. He wants you to experience true intimacy with Him—not just observe intimacy from others' time in His presence. He desires you to experience the fullness of relationship—not just a secondhand reflection of relationship through others' lives.

Sadly, under the grip of this struggle, our faith can become a spectator sport for our own counterfeit spiritual fix. And often, as a result, we'll flock to perverse displays of spiritual expression and false teaching because what is being said or done satisfies our feel-good senses and gives us an emotional high in the moment. But ultimately, we are not interacting personally in dynamic intimacy with our Bridegroom. Nor are we testing spirits with any prayerful discernment (1 John 4:1) because we struggle to know what the still, small voice of our Good Shepherd sounds like, leading us in the way we should go. And just as viewing porn often keeps a spouse out of the arms of the one they shared vows with, when our walk with the Lord becomes an observance of others' lives rather than a life-laid-down, cross-carrying, Spirit-filled reality, we miss the nearness and touch of God's presence in our own lives. No, God wants us to know true intimacy so we can engage and bear fruit of our own in this life.

3. Adulterous Hearts

Adultery is another sly and deceptive symptom we see manifest in both our physical and spiritual lives when we live by the flesh. It's absolutely damning to personal intimacy for both the adulterer and the partner who was wronged. It causes a deep wound that inhibits its victims from fully trusting the staying power and purity of God's love, keeping them apart from healing and revelation by His grace.

But as we discussed earlier, we all walk with adulterous postures in our flesh. And this is made evident by how emotionally lorded and self-centered we are. Jeremiah 17:9 says, "The heart is deceitful above all things, and desperately sick; who can understand it?" Those with adulterous hearts live pulled by the puppet strings of their feelings, their happiness, and their volatile, ever-changing mood toward the things of God. They forget the love for God and for others that they knew at first. The lure of sin leads to idolatry. Happiness is chosen over holiness. Excitement is chosen over investment. Lust is chosen over abiding love (Rom. 6:12). The things of the world and the voices, opinions, and interpretations of others are always in the mix. They live divided in loyalty and tossed like the waves of the sea.

> But when you ask him, be sure that your faith is in God alone. Do not waver, for a person with divided loyalty is as unsettled as a wave of the sea that is blown and tossed by the wind. Such people should not expect to receive anything from the Lord. Their loyalty is divided between God and the world, and they are unstable in everything they do. (James 1:6–8 NLT)

People with divided loyalty cannot expect to receive anything from the Lord. They are adulterous, unsettled, and unstable. And if their faith is split or seeks "balance" between the things of the world and the things of God, they cannot spiritually prosper.

We make gods of people and worship idols from the world based on the spikes and dips in our feelings at any given moment. Not only does this blind us to the staying, invested, deep-rooted truth of God's love (for He is *always* faithful to uphold His promises) but it also deceives us into believing we have the freedom to come and go as we please from the covenant made with Christ. As if our vows of faithfulness are subject to our evolving feelings. I find that many false, grace-abusing, and man-made doctrines are key contributors to coaxing people into spiritual apathy and, ultimately, spiritual adultery. Presuming we can come and go between the world and the Word as we please, as long as we recite a "sinner's prayer" at one sitting, is a dangerous theology. Marriage and intimacy do not work that way, physically or spiritually. And if we live that way, we will begin to perceive God's faithfulness as being just as flighty and fleeting as our own.

Matthew 19:6 makes clear, "So they are no longer two but one flesh. What therefore God has joined together, let not man separate." For a husband and a wife, as well as for Christ the Bridegroom and us, his bride, there is no walk in the fullness of the calling He has on our life and marriage and family if we have adulterous hearts. We cannot have a back-and-forth affection between other people and God—the world and the Word. There can be no other gods in the marriage bed, no idols, no stagnant stance in sin and compromise. Our spiritual intimacy must be pure. This is of utmost importance. Perhaps it's more important than we can really understand. We must have complete trust in the One we claim to know and follow. Our mantle and mission in life depend on our monogamous intimacy.

4. Shamelessness

Jeremiah 13:27 reads,

> People of Jerusalem, I have seen your adulterous worship, your shameless prostitution to, and your lustful pursuit of, other gods. I have seen your disgusting acts of worship on the hills throughout the countryside. You are doomed to destruction! How long will you continue to be unclean? (NET)

I deeply feel these words from the prophet Jeremiah, as I earnestly believe they point to the modern-day body of believers as well. We love to preach messages of Christ removing our shame, which carries truth in the proper context, but we fail to ever call out and call up the absolute shamelessness that is thick in the world and has infiltrated the modern "people of Jerusalem." The stench of our sin is thick in His temple, as a shameless approach to sex and intimacy—both physically and spiritually—is rampant. The brothel of this world has promoted and advertised an alluring norm of public "nakedness," exposure, and promiscuity. All void of modesty, commitment, and true connection. And the body of Christ has tolerated this compromise, inviting each other further into it and edifying each other's sin. Our apps coax us to pander our bodies for likes and shares. They loudly lure us into one-night stands and consumerism dating. We give away our bodies to whoever might affirm us, and the shamelessness of this popular and promoted practice deeply, deeply grieves my heart. Mainly because, if you have read my second book, *Sex, Jesus, and the Conversations the Church Forgot*, you know it was a lifestyle I lived for quite a while before truly understanding what it meant to live in obedience to God and, in view of His mercy, offer my body as a living sacrifice, holy and pleasing (Rom. 12:1).

This shamelessness we live shackled to deceives us to the nature of an honorable, holy, and dignifying God. We begin to believe that He is tolerant of our sin and, ultimately, we rationalize the respect He deserves. As well as the dignity He wants us to know as His creations. We see His character to be like that of our peers, vile and vying for us to immediately and explicitly expose ourselves in order to have value. We imagine He insists a shameless, immediate, and full disclosure of our deepest and most painful heart layers is necessary in order for Him to stay and care to be with us. That we must be stripped spiritually bare instantly—and that we will ultimately be exploited for being vulnerable with Him. That He'll get what He wants and go. This is just one of many things living in sync with a shameless culture deceives us to believe about intimacy with God, that His love is dependent on our performance. But performance-based showmanship is not true intimacy. Dignifying presence is. He does not shame us. Like Jesus did for the adulteress brought before him in John 8 to be stoned, He sees us exposed and dignifies us with His love.

5. Impure Marriage Beds

This shamelessness can also be seen through the perversion that has entered the marriage bed of many couples. Living apart from our heavenly Father, we are deceived to believe that just because we are married, we can engage in shameful, demoralizing, and perverse acts freely. This often leaves one or the other spouse feeling humiliated but unable to voice their feelings. And many things cultivated in such a marriage bed ultimately border on manipulation, abuse, and even rape. Just because you share a bed does not mean you can force yourself upon your partner without his or her heartfelt consent.

So often we carry into the marriage bed perverse things we learned from porn, shameless television, previous partners, or pandering movies. Rather than knowing the connection of face-to-face, heart-to-heart, mutually honoring intimacy, we've let the deceiver teach us that props and tools and man-made efforts to enhance our experience are appropriate. Of these things, God is in no way pleased. Hebrews 13:4 says, "Let marriage be held in honor among all, and let the marriage bed be undefiled, for God will judge the sexually immoral and adulterous."

Defiling and shameless acts within the covenant of marriage can also deceive us to believe we are just an object to God, unworthy of intimate dignity. Even within the gospel covenant, believing this physical lie prompts us to also believe in a spiritual union that is diminishing, debasing, forceful, void of communication, unsafe, and carnal in nature.

Sexual abuse and manipulation, whether we are married or unmarried, can give us the most damaging and improper view of God's invitation to intimacy. If someone has sinned egregiously by forcing themselves upon you, you likely perceive God as violent, manipulative, power hungry, and primed to conquer you. God's love is nothing like this—He is just and merciful, tender and patient. But perversion and trauma are deeply effective tools wielded by the enemy to blind us to the truth of God's nature.

Just because something is technically legal doesn't mean it's appropriate or beneficial. Just because you can bare your body on the internet or meet up with someone you swiped to connect with—or seemingly believe you can do whatever you want to and with your spouse's body—doesn't mean it's wise or edifying. Even if both parties claim to agree on certain things, it is still essential we bring each act to the throne and see if it aligns with God's heart for right-natured intimacy. For joy and expression and pleasure, of course, but within the confines of dignity, godly order, health, and honorable love. First Corinthians 10:23 reminds us that "'I have the right to do anything,' you say—but not everything is beneficial. 'I have the right to do anything'—but not everything is constructive" (NIV).

The lengths we can go to for shameless affirmation and connection reveal the wounds of a heart that does not realize it is being trafficked by a deceiver exploiting our true value, a deceiver who wants us to believe God does not see dignity in us, either.

6. Wounded Identities

According to the Scriptures, homosexuality is another sin struggle that manifests in the wounded hearts of those living oppressed by a hateful and manipulative enemy who is bent on deceiving humankind to their true, God-knit identity. Genesis 19:5, Leviticus 18:22 and 20:13, Deuteronomy 22:5, Judges 19:22–23, Romans 1:18–32, 1 Corinthians 6:9–11, and 1 Timothy 1:8–11 testify to homosexuality and express the full words and truth of Christ—who was and is and always will be unchanging.

I believe the greatest tactic of the enemy in this angle of attack is threefold: (1) to deceive God's incredible creations—both men and women alike—about their true identity as unique, dynamic, and inherently valuable image-bearing creations of God, (2) to confuse humankind to the absolute, unchanging nature of God's order and identity as Father, Son, Spirit, and as Bridegroom—head of the household that is His church, and (3) to ultimately escort the church into compromise and relativity, leaving our identity and assignment as His body open to the interpretation of humankind.

If the enemy can keep us chained in the brothel of our flesh, confused about our identity, God's identity, and the absolute nature of His ways, then he can effectively sterilize us—making us unable to reproduce physically or spiritually.

Homosexuality and all issues of identity confusion are struggles that disorient God's order and, thus, leave individuals uncertain about their personal identity and their role, godly function, and powerfully purposed place in the kingdom family. They effectively cause individuals to feel disconnected from the body they've been given and ill-fitting in the corporate body as well. This leaves us searching in manipulative and warped ways for what will ease the tension and disconnect we feel, as well as what will bring the understanding of identity and wholeness we are longing for. And rather than looking to, trusting in, and yielding completely to God's way of doing things, we are deceived to believe His ways are oppressive and that He is a liar—that His way is not the correct way but a way of bondage to the flesh rather than emancipation from its power. Spiritually disoriented yet longing for connectedness, understanding, and belonging, we then seek intimacy and communion with our own likeness. This ultimately escorts us away from exploring love, acceptance, and belonging through Christ and, instead, convinces us that our assuredness of identity is intended to come through other people.

The God of creation longs for us to know our true identity as sons and daughters of the Most High King, but the enemy would prefer we camp in the belief that God is a liar, a tyrant, prone to making mistakes, and untrustworthy—lest we discover we were made in the very image of our Maker and are empowered to annihilate the schemes of the deceiver when we rebuke the deception and sin in our lives.

Belief in the deep-rooted lie that God is oppressive by assigning identity and order not only leaves men rejecting their spiritual call toward godly masculinity, leadership, and authority but also emasculates the male and, spiritually, emasculates our understanding of Christ as Head of the church, full of authority over His bride. It rejects the righteous authority and the absolute nature of His truth and of His identity. And the church, the woman, is given to believe she was made to lead herself—to be both male and female, to lord and follow, to lead and submit. It leaves the body of Christ with the unbearable and ill-conceived thought that we must provide for ourselves and be strong enough to guide ourselves, protect ourselves, and write our own rules because certainly man—Christ—is not enough. Not sufficient. He must certainly be weak or abusive or apathetic. Unappealing and unattractive to our natural desire.

This robs us of the radical faith we are called to. It robs faith altogether. As women are left with no faith in men, so the church is left with no faith in Christ. When we do not believe He is a God of order, provision, protection, and perfect love, we do not assume the orderly role of reception, willingness to be protected, surrender, and radical trust. We become completely disoriented in our understanding of Christ as our Head and us, as the church, in willful submission to His lordship. And we live in direct opposition toward God's mandate—given for our ultimate good and for His glory—in the garden, because we distort our understanding of the absolute nature of God by believing it to be spiritually relative—defined by our ever-changing opinion. This manifests as humankind worshiping self and deciding for ourselves what we think is sin versus trusting in God's supremacy and our invitation to come under Him for our blessing.

As a result, we are deceived into compromise, tolerance, and relativity. We are lulled into believing there is a degree of tolerance, on God's part, for sin and immorality. That His holiness and His authority are subject to our interpretation. That His Word can be translated as we see fit—that it conforms to our desires—versus our yielding to His Word and being transformed by His truth. That the guiding determinants of what is sin and what is not are subject to our feelings—what feels good and what does not, what is satisfying versus what is not. God's nature becomes disordered and subject to our interpretation versus unchanging and sure. We begin to rationalize that our sinful nature is simply how we were made and how we will inevitably function all the days of our life. We become resolved that, no matter what our sinful dispositions are, we were "born this way" and therefore can completely reject the scriptural command that, in order to inherit the kingdom of heaven, we *all* must be born again. Instead, we become completely tolerant to the sin gripping our lives and the idolatrous nature of the heart rather than yielding to truth and learning we have the spiritual power and authority to call out sin for what it is, refuse to tolerate the oppression of the deceiver, and allow the very source of our heart struggles to be dealt with by the One who defeated the grave and holds perfect power over sin and death.

No matter what we desire to justify or how passionately we want to fight this truth, God is not subject to us; we are subject to Him. God is not malleable to our making; we are clay in the Potter's hand. But if the enemy can keep us confused and in a state of being constantly transient, he can keep us unfocused and unproductive for the kingdom of heaven here on earth.

We see this, for example, with many church models and denominations consistently trying to evolve and keep up with the culture—focusing more on relevance to the current worldly environment and thus emasculating the message from the pulpit and compromising absolute truth. Where the gathering of the fellowship should hold power, miraculous moves of God, and dynamic intimacy among spiritual family members gathered in full activation of their roles, gifts, and talents, it can instead look like a powerless performance for the masses, desperate to be received and loved but ultimately ineffective in cultivating depth and fruitful disciple-generating. How grieved God must be that His bride is confused about her identity.

We are being oppressed and deceived to believe we are the gods of our own stories—a curse that is burdensome, heavy, and deadly. But when we come to the revelation of the truth by the power of the Holy Spirit, and we engage our own free will to recognize His ways, His love, and His design are good, are better, and are worth exploring, we encounter true freedom. We discover a Bridegroom—Christ—who is perfectly sufficient in leading and providing. And a bride—the church—who lives in full trust and surrender under the protection and faithful provision of God.

When His love for us captures our hearts, disorder bends a knee to order. The faithless quick fix bends a knee to His faithful power at work. The spiritually wounded hear the still, small voice of a God who speaks true identity and healing over their stories. And the efforts of the enemy become crushed under the heel of an absolute God who reaches into the brothel and escorts out the oppressed into their true identities.

◦ ◦ ● ◦ ◦

So while, again, this is not an exhaustive list of physical struggles that reveal to us spiritual issues, it is a review of several prominent issues that I've seen result from life lived in the flesh, in the sinful world that moves under the authority of our greatest enemy. And, ultimately, it is a peek into the parallel that gives us spiritual insight. Revelation of ways in which we have been or actively are being deceived to believe false and damaging ideas about how God longs to commune with us.

In the midst of it all, our spirits are literally starving and crying out for intimacy. We were made to know God and to be fully known by God. But because the right-natured model of intimacy has been progressively warped, perverted, and manipulated . . . because perversion has been beautifully packaged to appeal to our flesh, our emotions, and our fallen desires . . . we struggle to understand why the brothel is not the place we are meant to be. The lusts of our flesh look and feel appealing, and they testify to the wickedness of our hearts that ultimately, pridefully, want to determine what is best for us, so we either hide from spiritual truth by isolating ourselves from being truly known by other believers, by stuffing conviction down, by avoiding situations and settings that would cultivate times of depth with the Lord, or by harboring an anger and resentment toward the "God" we perceive is "forcing us" to comply with His rigorous set of rules.

Or we run. We resolve to "move" and "go" and "do" at such a ceaseless pace that we never allow ourselves the time to stop and sit still with the One True God. We avoid Him by performing, by earning, by relentlessly going so we never have to sit down and get to know Him—lest intimate knowledge of Him coaxes our lives to transform. Lest His presence splay open our hearts to reveal the truth of our condition. Lest His presence incite a response that would cause us to show mercy and make sacrifices, to change direction, to deny ourselves, to humbly confess and take accountability for the fact that we regularly came into agreement with sin, that we spiritually welcomed the companionship of ungodliness time and time again. Instead we continue forward in our warped versions of intimacy and live in rhythm with counterfeit copies of His glory. We try to convince ourselves that immorality and the affirmations of others satisfy the deep parts of ourselves that are at war, internally. But it never measures up.

We justify everything as mere biological inclinations and physical inclinations—as if we are primitive animals ruled by the instincts of our flesh. But the truth is that all of these struggles root deeply at the heart level. First Corinthians 2:14 says, "The natural person does not accept the things of the Spirit of God, for they are folly to him, and he is not able to understand them because they are spiritually discerned." But if we dare to stop and sit still and seek to truly know God, He will help us understand that He does not simply want our behavior to change; He wants to minister to our hearts so that our whole lives transform. That we would come into the revelation that we are not just flesh and bones, subject to the culture of the brothel, but are meant to live in the freedom of His care because our hearts have been excavated, tended to, and resuscitated by His matchless mercy.

The truth is He loves us. He is a jealous God who loathes and detests sin because His anger burns toward the deceiver who seduced us out of His home and trafficked us mercilessly. He longs for His bride, and He will one day pour out wrath on the enemy for defiling His creations, as well as on all those who remain in unrepentant communion with darkness. But those who would arise from the sickbed and reach out to their Maker for salvation can find the truth and hope of God's immeasurable love. A love that is too great to contain, as His intimate love is *nothing like* these broken, counterfeit copies. The incredible truth of the gospel is that, despite our sin-prone flesh, easily deceived hearts, and spiritual adultery, in His infinite love and unfathomable mercy, God set out on a rescue mission to unshackle us from bondage and invite us out of false freedom into His right-natured, healing exchange.

Oh Abba,

Hear my cries. Hear the cries of my frustration, of my anguish, of my grief, and of the war taking place within me. Hear the cries of my flesh coming under submission to Your Word and Your Spirit. The shrieks of all the vicious agents working for the deceiver as they are exposed by Your light and drawn out to be seen—God, put them to death. Put every unclean spirit, every ruler, every principality to death within me. By the sword of Your Spirit, sever their heads. Cut off their very life source. God, it is not comfortable. It is not pleasant to see my own sin—whether it be revealed in the physical or the spiritual sense. It is painful to recognize the ways I've partnered with the deceiver because, ultimately, it has kept my heart in bondage, unable to rightly understand Your ways, Your love, Your nature, and Your truth. God, remove this heart of stone within me and replace it with a heart of flesh. Open my spiritual eyes that I would no longer live blindfolded by carnality. I know and believe that You are doing a good work—that

You want more for me, for others, for Your kingdom. That You long for us to know Your truth, because it is truth that ultimately sets us free. But sometimes that truth is really hard to receive. Comfort me, please. Counsel me. Anesthetize this heart surgery with Your tender mercy. Help me. I need You now more than ever. Give me the strength to press forward toward You.

Amen.

the marriage proposal

He didn't have to, you know.

Nothing obligated God, the One whom humankind sinned against, to extend mercy.

Nothing obligated God, the One whom you and I have mocked and denied, to extend grace.

What would warrant prison doors to be unlocked, an escape route made available to us "from the corruption that is in the world because of sinful desire" (2 Pet. 1:4)? What would warrant us to be chosen?

Certainly not our own righteousness. Certainly not any purity displayed that could earn rescue.

No, it could only be justice. Mercy. Compassion. Righteous anger against the deceiver. Jealousy. Grace. Love. That is what would compel a rescue mission.

> God so loved the world, that he gave his only Son, that whoever believes in him should not perish but have eternal life. For God did not send his Son into the world to condemn the world, but in order that the world might be saved through him. Whoever believes in him is not condemned, but whoever does not believe is condemned

already, because he has not believed in the name of the only Son of God. And this is the judgment: the light has come into the world, and people loved the darkness rather than the light because their works were evil. For everyone who does wicked things hates the light and does not come to the light, lest his works should be exposed. But whoever does what is true comes to the light, so that it may be clearly seen that his works have been carried out in God. (John 3:16–21)

And you were dead in the trespasses and sins in which you once walked, following the course of this world, following the prince of the power of the air, the spirit that is now at work in the sons of disobedience—among whom we all once lived in the passions of our flesh, carrying out the desires of the body and the mind, and were by nature children of wrath, like the rest of mankind. But God, being rich in mercy, because of the great love with which he loved us, even when we were dead in our trespasses, made us alive together with Christ—by grace you have been saved—and raised us up with him and seated us with him in the heavenly places in Christ Jesus, so that in the coming ages he might show the immeasurable riches of his grace in kindness toward us in Christ Jesus. For by grace you have been saved through faith. And this is not your own doing; it is the gift of God, not a result of works, so that no one may boast. For we are his workmanship, created in Christ Jesus for good works, which God prepared beforehand, that we should walk in them. (Eph. 2:1–10)

God the Father sent Christ, His Son, on mission to open the doors and encounter us, to pay a great and perfect price for us (1 Cor. 6:20), and to extend to us a better, renewed promise . . . for whosoever would accept it and hold fast to the commitment in preparation until He returns.

I will never forget the day Yeshua burst through the bars of my brothel stall and extended His powerful and yet perfectly kind mercy to my heart. I was imprisoned by hypocrisy, idolatry, deceit, anger, gluttony, fear, lust, and pride, and He was no respecter of persons, nor did He shame me due to the depth of my sin. My qualifying factor for needing to be saved was solely the evidence of my incarceration. And He came to set captives free.

Jesus's mercy in the hour I first came to believe, and His mercy every day moving forward as His love has refined and grown me—I see a reflection of it in the love I encountered in my husband Jeremiah's eyes when he asked me to be his bride. He looked at my past and took a knee for my future, and something about that kind of love is still just illogical to me.

It makes me think of Gomer, in the book of Hosea, who is referred to as "a wife of whoredom" (Hos. 1:2). What strikes me about the text is the love and faithfulness of Hosea, that he could not give her up. He could not hand her over without a fight. God is the Holy One in our midst, and Hosea's love of Gomer is, ultimately, redeeming love. Redeeming her value, her worth, her very identity as his wife. Such is God's love for us. For you. Passionate and illogical and redemptive. An extension of mercy that is intended to call us back into faithful commitment—honorable intimacy and obedience to His Spirit, propelled by His great love.

Why would we value any sin in our life, or the lure of false comfort in what we've always "known" and "done," if it hinders us from experiencing His heart, so rich in mercy? His Word says His mercies are new every morning, and He is always in the business of busting down doors for those who call on His name.

The Revelation of Redemption

If we are going to pour the foundations of our intimacy with God into the groundwork of His redeeming love, then we must know what redemption is and, in turn, what "redeeming love" genuinely means.

According to the *Oxford English Dictionary*, to *redeem* means to gain or regain possession of something in exchange for payment. And by biblical definition, it means to buy back, to save by payment of a ransom, and to free from the consequences of sin. To redeem something is to imply that it was, in fact, once deemed acceptable. At some point it became defiled, broken, fallen, and no longer acceptable. However, there was then a payment made to reclaim what was lost. To rescue, reconcile, and restore what—or I should say who—had wandered off. A payment made to redeem someone to their intended state, to the place he or she once began. Worthy and acceptable and holy in the eyes of a holy God. Intimate and communing together as intended.

When we look back to how things began in the garden, we see humankind's original, intended identity. And we can recognize that no matter where we are, who we are, what we are presently living in, what our circumstances are, or what has deceived and bound us, we were created by God and for God, for the glory of God. And while our sin defiled and continues to defile our intended holiness, the very nature of Yeshua's mission was to meet us right where we are, rebuke what is not of God, and redeem His creation—you and me. His task was to save us by the payment of His perfect, sinless life and buy back God's image bearers, freeing us from the active oppression and unfathomable consequences of sin. His life was a divine rescue mission that paid the price for our redemption and powerfully reveals to us the true nature of whom we are made to be: children of the Most High God.

God loves His people, and in His perfect, just love, He does not model or condone relative, opinionated, rationalized, or "comfortable" love. He invites those who truly want to know and be known by Him to repent of anything that is damaging, harmful, or compromising. His redeeming love invites us to turn away from the things that the deceiver has convinced us are fine, permissible, and even identity defining, and to turn our hearts back to our First Love.

Jesus did not come to redeem sin; He came to redeem the sinner. He rebukes the sin to redeem the God-created thing. Redemption and rationalized agreement are not the same thing. And it's important we remember that, because He wants us truly free from the things that hold us back from intimacy with Him. We must be willing to humbly acknowledge whatever in our lives is not aligned with His heart and His Word.

We can see this clearly when we look to the example of a strip club. Imagine you came upon a strip club and your goal was to redeem it for the glory of God. You would not come into the building in agreement with everything taking place there and simply stamp "Christ" on the front of the building, deciding that because you didn't want to cause too much offense or disruption, you would just call it a "Christian" strip club and leave things as they were. It would be irrational. Coming into agreement with something that is not of God for the purposes of "loving" people or keeping things "comfortable" would only be hypocritical and would still leave those sex slaves and workers imprisoned in their condition.

No! You would look to the function of the club and rightly understand the brokenness and exploitation and roots of darkness, pain, and perversion present. You would come on mission for the created things. You would come, in the name of Christ, for the redemption of the people and the restoration and repurposing of the building. Christ, your model whom you seek to be like, was never afraid to rebuke sin because He loved the vessel enough to do so, and so you would gut the place and restore it to function in an entirely new way—as a tool used for the glory, goodness, edification, and advancement of things pleasing in the eyes of God. You would tend to, provide for, speak truth over, and share the gospel with the women who once worked there, employing them in roles of dignity and honor within the new function of the redeemed space. And while their ultimate rehabilitation and healing would take time and come with layers that need to be slowly pulled back and wounds that must be carefully tended to, ultimately the efforts of teaching and relearning what it means to be truly free would hopefully prove to redeem and reorient their lives for greater glory.

This is the very nature of what His gospel intends to do in our hearts and our lives. He rebukes the filth, redeems His creation, and repurposes us with roles of power and purpose that align with the mission and heart of God. His redeeming love is intended to buy back the value, worth, and dignity we were always made to know.

The Proposal

First comes redeeming love, then comes marriage . . .

I find that one of the most beautiful ways we can see this gentle and generous element of the gospel come to life through the lens of intimacy is by looking at the components of an ancient Hebrew wedding.

In our modern culture, we can be viciously blinded to the goodness and beauty of God's invitation to spiritual intimacy when we liken it to how we go about singleness, engagement, and even marriage in a number of ways. So much brokenness has bled into the "Christian" courtship, wedding, and marriage model over time. And the greatest shame of that (though knowing we are in agreement with sinful practice should bring us to our knees in repentance all by itself) is we miss out on the beauty of what God always intended and how He reveals Himself through His biblical design.

We miss so much beauty, so much revelation of how He loves us and how the full and dynamic arc of the gospel is intended to be seen, when we look to an adulterous-hearted culture to set our rhythm for relationships. From a complete removal of parental involvement in the process of connecting with others, to virtual correspondence as our primary means of connection, to naked photos and physical perversion expected and "necessary" in a dating relationship, we are confronted immediately by environments and expectations that are not actually normal or healthy. From consumerism dating and carnally motivated pursuit, to one-night stands and a hookup culture, to long-term dating void of commitment, to cohabitation outside of marriage, we are constantly surrounded by brokenness and compromise as prerequisites for desirability. From the complete lack of understanding and celebration of the purpose and power in celibate, self-controlled singleness, to the gluttony and idolatry of commercialized weddings void of actual prayer and focus on the marriage, to the perversion of right-natured roles within marriage, to countless other broken, defiling, and gross "norms" in our modern relational pursuit, we've lost a lot.

It's no wonder the thought of intimacy with God is disconcerting. It's no wonder the gospel of Christ's work and invitation and ultimate promise is blurry to us. It's no wonder we're quick to believe He'll wound us, abandon us, force Himself upon us, or abuse us. Our understanding of intimacy is perverted from our warped experiences. We are looking at intimacy through mudsmeared goggles, though God wants to give us fresh sight.

When we look to the historical wedding customs of God's people, we find there is much to be discovered about Christ's love for us. We begin to understand how He pursued us, how He made a way for us to be unified, and why His invitation and the details of His promises and promised return are so heart-redefining. There are not enough pages in this book to break down the depth of divine detail woven together in ancient Hebrew weddings, as it could be an entire book on its own, but I do encourage you to separately study the intricate details of the customs of the very people Christ spoke to and shared life with in Galilee, and how they reveal Christ's first and second comings. This layer is not my own revelation; the sources are ample and intricate and not hard to find. What I simply want to show you, from a bird's-eye view, is how He invites us to true intimacy through the picture of union that He used to illustrate His design.

He First Chose You

> Therefore a man shall leave his father and his mother and hold fast to his wife, and they shall become one flesh. And the man and his wife were both naked and were not ashamed. (Gen. 2:24–25)

In ancient Hebrew wedding customs, we see this gospel invitation come to life. The first step in the marriage process was the common practice of the father's selection of a bride for his son. We see this when Abraham sent a representative to find a bride for Isaac in Genesis 24, just as we see this when God drew Eve from Adam's side. The same is true for Christ's bride; we are drawn from His side. Our invitation begins in knowing that God chooses us. He loves us. And He both makes us and saves us. The initiation of intimacy is His. John 15:16 says, "You did not choose me, but I chose you and appointed you that you should go and bear fruit and that your fruit should abide, so that whatever you ask the Father in my name, he may give it to you," and a similar statement is repeated in 1 Peter 2:9.

Deuteronomy 14:2 reads, "For you are a people holy to the LORD your God, and the LORD has chosen you to be a people for his treasured possession, out of all the peoples who are on the face of the earth." And Ephesians 1:3–6 reiterates,

> Blessed be the God and Father of our Lord Jesus Christ, who has blessed us in Christ with every spiritual blessing in the heavenly places, even as he chose us in him before the foundation of the world, that we should be holy and blameless before him. In love he predestined us for adoption to himself as sons through Jesus Christ, according to the purpose of his will, to the praise of his glorious grace, with which he has blessed us in the Beloved.

But perhaps this truth is most simply summarized in 1 John 4:19, as it is clear that, "We love because he first loved us." He truly loves us. He loves you. How miraculous and awe inspiring that He wants you.

The Bride Price

Just as the Scriptures show that the man left his father and mother's house, so Jesus left the heavenly realms for you. He traveled to His bride's home and was conceived by the Holy Spirit in the womb of a woman. The Son of God took on the flesh of man to attend our dwelling place.

Unlike Adam, who had not been able to resist Satan, Christ lived in perfect submission to God. Though bound by the same sin-prone, fallen flesh as you and me, He lived sinless in perfect obedience to the Father. Though tempted, tested, and tried (Matt. 4:1–11), Jesus yielded Himself completely to the point of death (Phil. 2:5–8). And while pride, disobedience, and control conquered Adam and brought death, Christ's perfect life of humility, obedience, and submission culminated in His rising from the dead and proving He was, in fact, supreme over sin and death. By faith in Him we too are not bound by the sinful pull of our temporary flesh but can crucify our flesh (Gal. 5:24) and come to spiritual life! By His power we can live in humility, submission, and obedience to God, just like Christ, operating in activation, purpose, and power by the Spirit, just like Christ.

In this act—living a sinless life and giving up His life by shedding His blood in order to be the pure, holy, and perfect atoning sacrifice for our sin—Christ's very life became our bride price (1 Pet. 1:18–19).

While it may seem strange or demeaning to consider a woman being "purchased" or "bought with a price," the truth is that in biblical times the pagan nations surrounding God's people practiced little to no means of dignifying or valuing women. If a man wanted a woman as his property, he could simply rape her and declare her to be his wife. But for His people, God put dignifying measures in place to honor women, standards set to protect and provide for them and make clear the measure of their worth and value in society. We see this through the story of Abraham's involvement with Isaac and Rebekah in Genesis 24, for instance. This *mohar*, or bridal price, was a gift paid by the groom that set his bride free from her parents' household and her father's authority.

What a gift, knowing that though in our sin we are "children of Satan," as explained in John 8:37–47, and ruled by our fallen form, "while we were still sinners, Christ died for us" (Rom. 5:8). God gave His Son, His very blood and life, to buy us from our "father's" house and redeem us by paying such a great and immeasurable price! The measure by which He values us is truly hard to understand. But there surely is no greater love than a man laying down His life for His friends (John 15:13) or a husband giving over his body for His wife (1 Cor. 7:4).

A Mutual Contract, Signed and Sealed

A fascinating portion of the Jewish bride and groom's preparation was a ritual immersion, or *mikvah*, in a pool of living, flowing water used for purification. This immersion, representing a spiritual cleansing, was done in preparation for the wedding ceremony and symbolized separating from an old life and beginning a new life—from life as single to life as married, a shift in identity and authority.

Christ was immersed in Matthew 3:13–17, and we too are immersed, by a washing of water with the Word (Eph. 5:25–27). This literal immersion in water symbolizes a spiritual immersion that cleanses away the impurities of the flesh. There is a shift in identity, as the old self has gone and the new has come.

Along with this *mikvah* was a very serious and very binding written legal agreement, or covenant, called the *ketubah*. Just as Yeshua specifically references the importance of what is written in Matthew 4, when the enemy is attempting to deceive Him by manipulating portions of God's Word, so the written element of this contract is powerful. It implies permanence and solidifies itself as a clear and unchanging reference point—just as the full Word of God is in our lives.

The *ketubah* was the marriage contract that solidified the betrothal, or engagement, and made promise for the future wedding of the bride and bridegroom after the engagement period was complete. This was a fascinating and dynamic five-part contract that aligned with the first five books of the Bible, the Torah. Thus, in the fullness of the Word, we can see that the Scriptures are a proclamation of love from Christ to His bride, beginning with a marriage contract with God's people . . . with you and me. You see, the *ketubah* was composed first of a detailed account of the origin and family history of the bride and groom (Genesis, the account of our creation). The second portion specified the history of the bride, including her genealogy and anecdotes of her family's history (Exodus, the history—our history—as God's people). Third was the history of the groom, including his genealogy and anecdotes of his family's history (Leviticus, the history of the Levites, God's chosen priests). And then came the telling of how the bride and groom met, complete with details of their relationship (Numbers, the telling of God's relationship with His people in the wilderness, full of dynamic description of His highs and lows as He pursued His love). And, lastly, the fifth section of the *ketubah* included details of the groom's and bride's specific duties in preparation for the marriage, as well as following the wedding (Deuteronomy, the details of what Christ and His bride were to fulfill). It outlines the couple's responsibilities for one another.

The New Testament, or *brit hadasha*, extends a renewed marriage covenant for all, Jew and gentile alike, who would turn their hearts to faith in Christ and commit to betrothal to the Bridegroom. When we study God's great love for us through this angle, we can see that biblical marriage, and Christ's "brit" with His church, are a culmination of these beautiful things, extended with even greater promise!

The new marriage covenant offered to you and me, in light of Christ's glorious love for us, is built on even greater promises than the old contract. Hebrews 8:6 makes this clear: "But as it is, Christ has obtained a ministry that is as much more excellent than the old as the covenant he mediates is better, since it is enacted on better promises." Not only does this marriage covenant invite us into His blessing, protection, provision, and eternal communion but our Bridegroom makes it clear that He will take God's laws, His ways, and His truths from simple written word and make them Spirit-breathed words inside of our hearts and minds (Heb. 10:16). Unveiling to us what the simple laws made for the flesh were seeking to teach our hearts, all brought to technicolor brilliance by the Spirit of God communing with us. Under His covenant, He promised to enter into us that we may know Him—know His thoughts and know His heart—even now and then forevermore. The spirit of the physical laws will come alive to us in understanding and completely transform our hardened hearts, equipping us with matchless power and inviting us to humble obedience to His Spirit.

● ● ● ● ●

What's really interesting about the *ketubah* is that it ultimately implied an ongoing relationship with no appointed end that was mutual—meaning it stipulated the groom's commitment to support, love, and provide for his bride as well as the bride's commitment to pay her dowry and prepare herself. A dowry was what the bride committed to bring into the covenant from her side, usually in the form of financial contribution. From the groom's side, once this contract was signed and sealed, he was completely committed. The bride, on the other hand, promised to pay her dowry but could freely choose to back out of the agreement at any time, up until the betrothal was fully consummated after the time of engagement.

Our dowry, as Christ's church, is intended to be the commitment of our yielded life, submitted will, and full heart to love Him alone and forsake all others. While Christ has fully committed Himself to us through the engagement process, we must pay our dowry of giving Him our lives completely and be sure we do not forsake Him, abandon the covenant we make with Him, or choose apostasy, denial, or blasphemy of the Holy Spirit as we await His return. Again, free will is necessary for true love and intimacy, and the free will we carry is essential in the Christ-betrothed life.

Yes, despite the marriage being arranged by the groom's father, the consent of the bride to agree to the *ketubah* was essential (Gen. 24:5). The marriage contract was a binding agreement that required mutual consent—just as our profession of faith, our betrothal to Christ, is an agreement requiring mutual consent.

The offer of salvation is extended to you and me through Christ, and our bride price was fully paid by Him on the cross. The choice before us is if we will open the door to Him (Rev. 3:20), bring our dowry of a fully submitted life, and choose to be transformed, be prepared, and remain faithful until His return. When we confess with our mouth and believe in our hearts that He is who He says He is and He will be fully faithful to do what He says He is going to do, we will be saved (Rom. 10:9), because it is His love that woos us into upholding our mutual commitment over time—His Spirit that ultimately keeps us in His love. Legal justification comes when we agree to His *ketubah* by His blood; it is His contract stating what is at hand and what is promised to come in the future.

Gifts before Departing

The next portion of the ancient Hebrew wedding is perhaps my favorite portion to reflect on, as it is the very thing that enables the intimacy, or *yada*, assured in the covenant. To truly know Him and to be known by Him is the power of what Christ extended to us, His betrothed, before He departed.

When all was publicly agreed upon and the bridegroom and bride confirmed their covenant by sharing a cup of wine, their commitment to one another was expressed and there was a sharing of items of significance, thus making the betrothal complete. It was then the couple was considered formally "married."

However, this betrothal period was to last for a year, in which the groom departed to prepare a place in his father's house, the couple did not formally consummate their marriage or live together, and the bride was responsible for preparing herself and her bridal wear. Joseph and Mary were in this period of preparation and betrothal when Jesus was conceived and born, hence Mary was still a virgin and Joseph had not yet "known" her, as the Scriptures say.

During the betrothal period, the Hebrew groom was to uphold his promises of going and preparing a place for his bride that was better than what she had come from and was entirely dependent upon his father's approval before he could return to receive her. There are unbelievable parallels to the gospel through this process! We see this in Christ's words:

> "Let not your hearts be troubled. Believe in God; believe also in me. In my Father's house are many rooms. If it were not so, would I have told you that I go to prepare a place for you? And if I go and prepare a place for you, I will come again and will take you to myself, that where I am you may be also. And you know the way to where I am going." Thomas said to him, "Lord, we do not know where you are going. How can we know the way?" Jesus said to him, "I am the way, and the truth, and the life. No one comes to the Father except through me. If you had known me, you would have known my Father also. From now on you do know him and have seen him." (John 14:1–7)

Also, in Mark 13:32–33 He said, "But concerning that day or that hour, no one knows, not even the angels in heaven, nor the Son, but only the Father. Be on guard, keep awake. For you do not know when the time will come."

Before Jesus ascended to heaven to fulfill His promise in returning to His Father's house to prepare a place for us, He left for His bride the promise of a gift that would be sent. After the profession of our faith, there is a union of spirits. Two become one, and we receive the Holy Spirit (Acts 2:38). The *matan*, or bridal gift, for Christ's bride is the gift of the Holy Spirit. This gift of Himself— His power, His Spirit—to be poured out within us is the greatest gift Christ gives His bride. This baptism by fire, this precious gift, is the same Spirit poured out at Pentecost (Acts 2:1–4) and is now poured out into you and me. He serves many purposes, but perhaps the most beautiful one is as a tangible pledge of His love for us and His power we can know and actively experience and participate with, which remind us of His faithfulness.

Ephesians 1:13–14 says, "In him you also, when you heard the word of truth, the gospel of your salvation, and believed in him, were sealed with the promised Holy Spirit, who is the guarantee of our inheritance until we acquire possession of it, to the praise of his glory."

And what is profound is that the gift of the Holy Spirit is dynamic and multilayered. A gift containing countless more gifts that are revealed throughout our betrothal time, just a few of which are words of wisdom, words of knowledge, faith, healing, miracles, prophecy, discernment of spirits, kinds of tongues, and the interpretation of tongues. The Spirit also bears the fruit of love, joy, peace, forbearance, kindness, goodness, faithfulness, and self-control. One and the same Spirit works all these things, distributing to each one individually as He wills (1 Cor. 12:8–11; Gal. 5:22–23).

His Spirit, His power, brings us to life and serves many essential purposes in the time we are here on earth, before our Bridegroom returns to complete the marriage and consummate—or perfect—us completely.

Preparation Time

What came next in the ancient Hebrew wedding is where we stand now, at present, in our time on earth before Christ returns for us. It is the meat of how physical intimacy, I believe, reveals gospel truth. The time between the groom's departure and his return, as the bride awaited him, was and is a period of *kiddushin*, or sanctification.

The bride entered a season of time in which she was to be set apart from the world, sanctified and in preparation. So we too, the bride of Christ, must be fully focused and intent on making ourselves ready for our Bridegroom's return to receive us. We must know true and transformational intimacy with God, one of the primary missions of the Holy Spirit in our lives, so that we are ready when He returns; we are set apart, being made holy and pure.

Ephesians 5:25–27 says, "[Christ] gave up his life for [the church] to make her holy and clean, washed by the cleansing of God's word. He did this to present her to himself as a glorious church without a spot or wrinkle or any other blemish. Instead, she will be holy and without fault" (NLT). Revelation 3:4 guides us toward this intimate and dynamic interaction with the Holy Spirit in reminding us we must be people who have not soiled our garments but who will "walk with [Him] in white." In this time of sanctification by the Holy Spirit we are, from whatever state we are currently in, to be washed in Christ's blood through His death (Rev. 7:14) and kept pure as virgins through sanctification by his Spirit (14:4).

But how do we do this? What does intimacy with the Holy Spirit look like? What model can we look to for help in understanding sanctification and the power of the Holy Spirit's purpose in our lives? The completion of the ancient Hebrew wedding includes the return of the bridegroom and, ultimately, the marriage feast that is still to come, but as we'll discuss later, physical intimacy is a prophetic picture God has given us to look to in order to understand the consecrating power of the Holy Spirit in our lives.

Father,
You are holy and You are kind. Hallowed be Your name. I praise You and thank You for Your love. I praise You, Father,

for choosing me. I praise You, Jesus, for the incredible bride price You paid for my life. I thank You, Lord, for Your Holy Spirit. What a beautiful gift. Thank You, God, for the revelation of Your gospel through the covenant You extended to me. Thank You for not only rescuing me from the brothel of sin but also extending Your dignifying mercy and grace over my life. Lord, I marvel that You would see the adulteress and extend redeeming love. And not only that, but that You would extend a renewed marriage proposal to me! I praise You. Empower me by Your Spirit to cherish the covenant made. Empower me by Your Spirit to bring the dowry of my fully yielded life to You for the remainder of my days. Empower me by Your Spirit to fully understand the call to preparation as I await Your return. Please teach me, speak to me, and lead me in the way I should go from this day forward. You are mine and I am Yours.

    Amen.

the hidden place

It's not talked about enough.

Repentance.

Sanctification.

Holiness.

The call to a set-apart life.

Sadly, we've removed these words from much of modern American Christianity. But just because they are not on the lips of popular pastors and appeasing pulpits doesn't mean they have been removed from the one true gospel of salvation.

Jesus paid the bride price of His life to free us from the power of sin's grip on us (Gal. 5:1), but what makes that price incomprehensibly valuable in our lives is our recognition of how desperately grateful we are for it. Because we recognize how desperately we need it. How hopeless our state is within the brothel of our sin and flesh, and how unfathomably kind, patient, and forbearing He is to extend to us mercy from His wrath (Rom. 2:4). Because apart from that choosing by the Father, apart from that sacrifice of the Bridegroom's life, apart from the rescue mission of heaven to redeem His created beings and rebuke the sin that for so long has held a vise grip on us, we are hopeless. Trapped. Separated from the One we were made to know. I praise God for His mercy and His saving love. How devastating it would be to see an open door and extended arm reaching out to offer us rescue yet choose to stay in bondage. It is His kindness, after all, that leads us to repentance (Rom. 2:4). His patience and mercy that meet us in our pain and dignify us with an invitation home.

The very equation Peter provides when Pentecost was at hand and the rich nature of God's gift of the Spirit was being poured out—when people were pierced to their core in revelation of Jesus as the Son of God and asking how and what they should do in response—is the same cry of the prophets, of John the Baptist, of the Messiah Himself: repent of your sins and turn back to God!

> [Peter] answered them, "Turn from sin, return to God, and each of you be immersed on the authority of Yeshua the Messiah into forgiveness of your sins, and you will receive the gift of the *Ruach Ha-Kodesh* [Holy Spirit]! For the promise is for you, for your children, and for those far away—as many as ADONAI our God may call!" He pressed his case with many other arguments and kept pleading with them, "Save yourselves from this perverse generation!" So those who accepted what he said were immersed, and there were added to the group that day about three thousand people. (Acts 2:38–41 CJB)

The beauty of what this shows is that repentance is an active verb. It is not just apologizing and asking for forgiveness. It is not just hating the consequences of sin and wanting a clear conscience. It is not just confessing to someone and hoping that is enough to feel better. No, these things are just worldly grief. Grief of the flesh that, ultimately, is incomplete and still produces death. Rather, repentance is marked by a godly sorrow that leads us to a *change* in direction, to turning away from sin and toward righteousness.

For godly grief produces a repentance that leads to salvation without regret, whereas worldly grief produces death. For see what earnestness this godly grief has produced in you, but also what eagerness to clear yourselves, what indignation, what fear, what longing, what zeal, what punishment! At every point you have proved yourselves innocent in the matter. (2 Cor. 7:10–11)

Repentance implies a move. A return. A return to the garden. A return to our true identity. To our true Father. To our one true love. Godly sorrow is driven by the realization that we grieved His heart in settling for anything less than Him. That we defiled our temples with sin. That we ever came into agreement with the very things that held us in enmity toward Him. Godly sorrow compels us to return . . . to change our mind. To crucify our flesh with Christ (Gal. 2:20) and go and sin no more (John 8:11). To truly be transformed. Anything less than transformation is not true repentance prompted by His Spirit. Turning away from sin and back to God bears fruit. His gospel meets us wherever we are, right where we are—but it absolutely refuses to leave us the same.

Repentance is not a scary or shameful word; it is the heart cry of the gospel! It is the voice crying out in the wilderness for us to turn *away* from our flesh and *back* to God in order to find spiritual life. Don't just apologize for adultery and continue forward. Feel the godly grief of your agreement with darkness, receive God's unfathomable mercy to forgive you of your sin, and walk forward in righteousness, in pace with the bold and beautiful stride you were always made to know! He has made a way through Christ. And He will give you the greatest gift in helping you as you navigate this world moving forward.

Filled with the Spirit as a gift from the lover of our souls, we now stand in the middle ground. Between commitment and consummation. We stand in the midst of the preparation. And in that preparation period of power and kingdom come, an essential layer of our lives in covenant with Christ is our sanctification. Our purification. Our all-consuming journey of spiritual maturity, so we can be made wise and ready, set apart and alert, eager and longing for our Bridegroom's return.

◦ ◦ ◉ ◉ ◦

Just as repentance is not a suggestion but a command, so sanctification too is an essential layer of our lives. Compelled and sustained by His unfathomable love for us, by God's life-surrendered, sacrificial, vast, and immeasurable love for us. Hebrews 12:14 is just one of many clear instructions in this truth, as it reads, "Pursue . . . sanctification without which no one will see the Lord" (NASB). The ESV version reads, "Strive for . . . holiness without which no one will see the Lord."

And Romans 6:22 also makes clear, "But now that you have been set free from sin and have become slaves of God, the fruit you get leads to sanctification and its end, eternal life."

Yet for some reason many are unfamiliar with this scriptural layer of the gospel message. Many turn a blind eye to the Holy Spirit altogether, which is extremely disconcerting, as reception of the gift of the Holy Spirit is absolutely fundamental to the faith. After all, in John 3 we see Jesus explicitly tell Nicodemus that no one can enter the kingdom of God unless he or she is born of the Spirit. The Holy Spirit gives birth to spiritual life. Not just a baptism by water but a baptism by fire (Matt. 3:11). Refining, empowering, faith-igniting fire within you!

And many also turn a blind eye to one of the primary assignments of the Holy Spirit in a believer's life: to progress forward in actively convicting us of sin (John 16:7–8). That is one of the most powerful functions of the Spirit in us, and one that I am most grateful for! The Holy Spirit is our deposit guaranteeing our inheritance until redemption comes (Eph. 1:13–14); the Holy Spirit unveils our eyes to the spiritual realm (2 Cor. 3:16), helps us, teaches us, reminds us of God's Word (John 14:26), guides us in all truth, declares to us the things to come (16:13–15), helps us when we are weak, and intercedes in prayer through us according to the will of God (Rom. 8:26–27). The Holy Spirit also searches our hearts and minds, gives us divine revelation in conjunction with the wisdom and thoughts of God (1 Cor. 2:9–11), gives spiritual gifts to believers (12:7–11), sanctifies us, makes us holy, and enables us to bear good fruit!

Romans 8:16–17 reminds us, "The Spirit himself bears witness with our spirit that we are children of God, and if children, then heirs—heirs of God and fellow heirs with Christ, provided we suffer with him in order that we may also be glorified with him." But navigating ongoing, refining conviction of sin, humbling ourselves in recognition of our sin, continuing to rhythmically repent, and yielding our flesh and often suffering in the flesh for the sake of the gospel make us uncomfortable.

I think we often prefer a grace-abusing message that tickles our ears and keeps us content because it feels safe. It feels good. It allows us to pick up and carry a cross of our own making that's not all that heavy. It allows us to consider ourselves crucified with Christ without really dying. It allows us to think we can reap the eternal benefits of heaven without looking like Christ in making the earthly sacrifices of our desires and our flesh in order for our spirit to rise. The thoughts of sin and hell and the need for purification and preparation are ultimately scary, so we dismiss any talk of colaboring efforts with Christ as "works based" or "legalistic" rather than holding fast to the many active verbs in the New Testament addressing the body of Christ that encourage us to "strive," "throw off," "cleanse ourselves," "flee," and more.

But Philippians 2:12–16 reminds us,

> Therefore, my beloved, as you have always obeyed, so now, not only as in my presence but much more in my absence, work out your own salvation with fear and trembling, for it is God who works in you, both to will and to work for his good pleasure. Do all

things without grumbling or disputing, that you may be blameless and innocent, children of God without blemish in the midst of a crooked and twisted generation, among whom you shine as lights in the world, holding fast to the word of life, so that in the day of Christ I may be proud that I did not run in vain or labor in vain.

Unfortunately, while our heavenly Father invites us to a stunning, awe-inspired, prostrating fear that is intertwined with honor and reverence, there is a deceptive and perverse brand of fear that the deceiver has rooted deep into our hardened hearts. This fear ultimately testifies to the fact that our understanding of progressive sanctification, holiness, and a set-apart life have not been made perfect in love. First John 4:16–18 says,

So we have come to know and to believe the love that God has for us. God is love, and whoever abides in love abides in God, and God abides in him. By this is love perfected with us, so that we may have confidence for the day of judgment, because as he is so also are we in this world. There is no fear in love, but perfect love casts out fear. For fear has to do with punishment, and whoever fears has not been perfected in love.

This process of having faith in the grace of Christ, yielding to the Holy Spirit, repenting of sin, and enduring to the end as we are being made complete in Him is profoundly beautiful. It is the steak our hungry souls long for in feasting with the Lord. It is the antithesis of the grace-abusing crackers we've been fed for far too long and left starving and unsatisfied by. Recurring and consecrating communion with the Holy Spirit is the very matter of substance in our intimate relationship with God, and it is what steadily transforms us into His image and likeness.

To deny His invitation to a rhythm of repentance in our lives and the continual work of sanctification because we have allowed fear to paralyze us is to come under curse when we commune with Christ. First Corinthians 11:27–32 so beautifully reminds us,

Whoever, therefore, eats the bread or drinks the cup of the Lord in an unworthy manner will be guilty concerning the body and blood of the Lord. Let a person examine himself, then, and so eat of the bread and drink of the cup. For anyone who eats and drinks without discerning the body eats and drinks judgment on himself. That is why many of you are weak and ill, and some have died. But if we judged ourselves truly, we would not be judged. But when we are judged by the Lord, we are disciplined so that we may not be condemned along with the world.

Romans 12:3 states, "For by the grace given to me I say to everyone among you not to think of himself more highly than he ought to think, but to think with sober judgment, each according to the measure of faith that God has assigned."

To live in awareness of and submission to the Spirit's continual work of sanctification and purification in our lives is to live earnestly and honestly, allowing the work of the Lord in us to be achieved, even if that process is humbling and at times hard. It is ultimately holy. It progressively transforms us and empowers us, maturing us in relational depth and dependence on the One we were made to know. Empowering us to a greater and greater degree as we make ourselves more and more available for His dynamic use in the world.

As Philippians 1:6–11 reads,

I am sure of this: that the One who began a good work among you will keep it growing until it is completed on the Day of the Messiah Yeshua. It is right for me to think this way about you all, because I have you on my heart; for whether I am in chains or defending and establishing the Good News, you are all sharing with me in this privileged work. God can testify how I long for all of you with the deep affection of the Messiah Yeshua. And this is my prayer: that your love may more and more overflow in fullness of knowledge and depth of discernment, so that you will be able to determine what is best and thus be pure and without blame for the Day of the

Messiah, filled with the fruit of righteousness that comes through Yeshua the Messiah—to the glory and praise of God. (CJB)

Right-natured intimacy between a husband and a wife provides a picture of this rich and layered element of our faith, but I believe we fear sanctification because we perceive God's dealings with us through perverted and vile relational lenses.

I will reiterate again that the Holy Spirit's interactions with us are nothing like the brokenness you may have experienced with other people. God will not force Himself upon you, defile you, or aggressively dominate you. Intimacy with the Holy Spirit is nothing like the fleeting and fake lusts of humankind. He does not leave us in humiliating uncertainty, manipulating our emotions and toying with our hearts, faithful one minute and flighty the next. Coaxing us in and then rejecting us when the layers and depths of our humanity are exposed. Intimacy with God is not belittling, incessantly forcing us to "prove ourselves" in order to be acknowledged. He does not tease or taunt. He is not aloof or arrogant, bullying us with reminders of our inadequacy or taunting us with worry that we may not be smart enough to figure Him out or skilled enough to keep His attention. He does not wield the "silent treatment" as a means of manipulating us and forcing us to grovel, nor does He insist we entertain Him to keep Him satisfied.

That does not mean God is moldable to our own making. He is not an emasculated leader, easily impressionable, feeble, or powerless. He is a God of love and mercy and a God of justice and wrath. He is not confused about His supremacy, His identity, or His absolute authority. He is not apathetic or slothful, nor is He able to be manipulated or mocked. The Father is the Judge in complete control of our eternal existence—whether that be in eternal communion with Him or cast into the lake of fire where there is both weeping and gnashing of teeth. God is very much holy and still very much the God of the Old Testament. Unchanging. He is the One who was and is and is to come.

What is profound about His nature, in light of these things, is that He loves us so much He exercises His authority in perfect patience, kindness, humility, gentleness, forbearance, peace, and endurance. God's dealings with us are those of a sober-minded and steady husband. His love for us encompasses completely the roles of perfect Master, Friend, and Father. He fills every role with excellence, and every hole of inequity in our lives overflows with His identity and invitation over us. His strength and authority pulse in rhythm with gentleness and honor. His correction and rebuke are served with His faithfulness and comfort. He loves us and is absolutely monogamous, loyal, and committed to uphold His promises and keep His Word.

Christ is not an adulterous Bridegroom, and His invitation to us is that we would live a yielded life, empowered by His Spirit and by His great and perfect love, in order to be a monogamous and faithful bride. That we would love God with all of our heart, soul, strength, and mind (Deut. 6:4–7; Matt. 22:37–40; Mark 12:30–31; Luke 10:27). That we would have no other gods before Him and that our yes to Him would thus be a no to all others. We forsake and renounce all other idols, false gods, and temporary fixes in order to truly walk in committed and pure monogamy with our One True Love (Luke 14:33). And, as 2 Corinthians 7:1 makes so profoundly clear, "Because we have these promises, dear friends, let us cleanse ourselves from everything that can defile our body or spirit. And let us work toward complete holiness because we fear God" (NLT).

So, the question then stands, If one of the primary jobs of the Holy Spirit dwelling within us is to walk with us, transform our hearts, convict us of sin, and actively sanctify and make us holy, where does that begin? And where does that continue to occur?

Holy Work in Quiet Caves

I remember when my husband and I exchanged vows, and our covenant to one another was sealed with a holy kiss. All we longed to do from that moment forward was to steal away together into seclusion. Into privacy. Into our own intimate hiding place.

Our love for one another and our heartfelt, monogamous commitment set a fire within us and cultivated an almost inexplicable desire for oneness and connection on every level—physical, mental, emotional, and spiritual. There was a deep hunger within both of us to turn away from the world and delight in the mystery of passionate communion.

A removal to a hidden place.

I experienced the same need to steal away when I first came to faith.

Just as the bridal chambers and the honeymoon suite are cherished as sacred, intimate spaces, so too are the hidden places in our faith. The unseen, private spaces we escape to in order to commune with the One whom our soul loves. To pray. To digest His Word. To intercede. To wrestle. To rest with Him. To simply be. To be one.

The spirit of the law makes sense in Deuteronomy 24:5, when God designed separation from duties for a newly married couple: "When a man is newly married, he shall not go out with the army or be liable for any other public duty. He shall be free at home one year to be happy with his wife whom he has taken." A God-granted right to cease striving in order to delight in covenantal union—what a gift. One He is also speaking to the Bridegroom and His bride. *Go away for a while. Nurture the joy of your union. Know one another, in all the many ways you've never known one another before.*

This season in the unseen, hidden place of our hearts is often so rich when we first come to believe. We hunger for His Word; we find ecstasy in the revelation that He sees us just as we are and draws near. We pray fervently and frequently when we come to realize that He hears us—and that He responds! We cherish the hidden place. But what we must remember is that this is not just a one-time thing. It is not just a single season of zeal, though the busyness of life often serves to keep us out of our Lover's arms. The honeymoon is by no means the only time a husband and wife come together, and so it is with us and God. Spouses grow and learn about one another and share dynamic intimacy as they find a rhythm to their union, consistently coming back together and growing in love.

Retreating from the world to commune with God is intended to be desirable, frequent, and honorable in privacy. Between a husband and a wife, as well as between Christ and His bride, intimacy should be cherished and guarded as sacred with ultimate discretion—just as the Holy of Holies was cherished and guarded as sacred behind the veil in the temple. Others should not see, hear, or be salaciously told about what occurs between a husband and wife in the confines of their communion, and the Word reinforces the same for much of what God does in and through us in the quiet places where we draw near to Him.

> And when you pray, you must not be like the hypocrites. For they love to stand and pray in the synagogues and at the street corners, that they may be seen by others. Truly, I say to you, they have received their reward. But when you pray, go into your room and shut the door and pray to your Father who is in secret. And your Father who sees in secret will reward you. (Matt. 6:5–6)

The vast majority of a believer's life, faith, and sanctification is cultivated in the hidden place. God does holy work in quiet caves, if only we'll steal away with Him for a while. If only we'll steal away with Him incessantly—if we'll pray without ceasing, commune with Him continually (1 Thess. 5:16–18), meet Him where He is waiting for us, enticing us to come away into His love.

I remember, so clearly, when He whispered that word to my heart. I had a baby crying to nurse, a toddler fussing at the table, construction workers sawing tile as they labored to reconstruct our flooded and gutted home, dogs whining to be let out, and a microwave incessantly beeping to remind me my breakfast was getting cold.

I was sitting on the kitchen floor, crying, when I tangibly felt His touch and heard His whisper, *I do holy work in quiet caves.* These caves can be real, intentional, and tangible, as well as caves of life that are seasonal.

I think of the virgin Mary, birthing heaven down to earth in that dark and musty cave in Bethlehem, and the inexplicable miracles that are knit together in every mother's womb. I think of the spirit of revival He once sent coursing through my heart while I was holed up in an ICU room with my tiny baby fighting for her life.

I think of the quiet cave of a prayer closet, a daily commute, the shower, an office cubicle, even facedown by the bedside. The cave of a house for the stay-at-home mom where she lays down her life every minute of every day, the caves of wilderness He draws us through as we follow Him and step away from the world, the caves of "invisibility" in our lives, our seasons of life that feel mundane or thankless or tiresome or repetitive.

The quiet cave of our hearts as He dwells within us and ministers to us with every pulse and pump. The quiet, unseen, uncelebrated, unassuming places in which our plans and our pride take a seat just long enough for His still, small voice to be heard. It's in these spaces that He unpacks His power and reveals more of Himself to us—if we stop despising the unseen life and value it rightly for all it is eternally worth.

Our culture mocks these caves, like they aren't enough or aren't valuable and important places to be. And, on top of that, our flesh coaxes us to make the intimacy exchanged in private a far more public thing. Let the world see how godly you are—if the Lord shares a word with you, share it publicly! If He points out a sin in you, He wants you to disrobe and make sure everyone immediately knows you're growing! If He prompts you to generosity, be sure others know exactly what you've given and who you've given it to!

But wait—is this the Father's way of faith, or the former exploitive way of the brothel?

> Beware of practicing your righteousness before other people in order to be seen by them, for then you will have no reward from your Father who is in heaven. Thus, when you give to the needy, sound no trumpet before you, as the hypocrites do in the synagogues and in the streets, that they may be praised by others. Truly, I say to you, they have received their reward. But when you give to the needy, do not let your left hand know what your right hand is doing, so that your giving may be in secret. And your Father who sees in secret will reward you. (Matt. 6:1–4)

Publicly baring all—isn't that what our flesh wants? The rush. The likes. The attention our bodies and sexuality can bring us. How disconcerting that this is reflected in our spiritual lives as well. This was a hard lesson I learned only by God pointing it out to me as I went through the process of truly learning what intimacy with Him meant. It was agonizing to see how I had lived like Balaam does in Numbers 22–24, going ahead of God with my own agenda and chasing what was offered by the world. I was sharing everything I received from Him with the world without intimately and privately applying it to my own life first. Missing the value of the Lord's pace is a death sentence to spiritual sustainability.

While our culture invites us to disregard the sanctity of the quiet, unseen places and instead bare all of our pearls at all times for all the swine to see, I believe God is inviting us to begin and persist in primarily private intimacy. After all, is that not the divine pace and rhythm we saw in the life of the Messiah? Jesus frequently and adamantly withdrew to the wilderness to be alone with His heavenly Father. Remember when He fed the five thousand? In that moment, they wanted to exalt Him as king. But what did He do? He "withdrew again to the mountain by himself" (John 6:15). Jesus lived in sync with His Father, and fiercely prioritized intimacy and communion over elevation and exposure throughout His ministry.

The way of our Bridegroom looks different from the way of the world. The holy work in quiet caves is where we learn humility. These caves, no matter how unassuming they seem, are where He pours out His divinity. If only we'll learn to retire to the master suite, lock the doors, and stand eye to eye with the One whom we are invited to delight in and, by that delight, gradually be transformed.

The Undressing

There is a lot of vulnerability found in the silence of two lovers, eye to eye, face-to-face, heart-to-heart. When, as a bride, I went with my husband to the unseen place and closed the door, there was a moment where things were so quiet all I could hear was my own heart pounding. A breathlessness like that which comes in the presence of a holy encounter. Do we still feel the awe of God's invitation to communion?

Then there is the cultivation of conversation. Communication is undoubtedly an essential part of any relationship, and when right-natured communication is cultivated in the bedroom, safety, assuredness, and dignity are formed. And spiritually, this is often the way of the unseen place too. An invitation to awe followed by a comfort that cultivates conversation as we catch our breath and find our voices. The unseen place is where the prayers pour out. Where our voices lift in our prayers and supplications, our desires (which can be dynamic and changing), and our thanksgiving.

It's where we bring our petitions and fears and full humanity. It's where we grieve and lament and cry out to God. Those words can sometimes be concise and clear, as Matthew 6:7–8 reminds us, "And when you pray, do not heap up empty phrases as the Gentiles do, for they think that they will be heard for their many words. Do not be like them, for your Father knows what you need before you ask him." In other circumstances, when the conversation cultivated in that space is deeper and harder and beyond our understanding, He holds us and intercedes on our behalf, finding the very words for us.

> Likewise the Spirit helps us in our weakness. For we do not know what to pray for as we ought, but the Spirit himself intercedes for us with groanings too deep for words. And he who searches hearts knows what is the mind of the Spirit, because the Spirit intercedes for the saints according to the will of God. (Rom. 8:26–27)

And then comes the very thing that makes communion with the Holy One of Israel so set apart: the fact that He responds. Our beloved God talks back to us if we'll simply pause and listen for a while. Sometimes when we withdraw to the unseen place, we end up talking our Bridegroom's ear off and then getting up to leave before even pausing to hear a response. My husband, Jeremiah, knows all too well that this is a poor habit of mine, so I speak from experience on what I've learned from this error. Intimacy can't be cultivated by steamrolling our lover. No, the unseen places aren't to be filled with words and then abandoned, but rather we take a posture of pause to hear from the One who loves our time together and delights in responding.

"Speak, for your servant is listening" (1 Sam. 3:10 NIV). That's how I've learned to end my words, and I've discovered His ways and His voice all the more clearly. With that prayer, I always encounter a faithful response. In fact, if there is anything I've learned most powerfully in exploring what it means to know and be known fully, it is that the Spirit of the Living God will become very clear and very loud when we are willing to become very quiet and very small.

This is where His sanctifying voice begins to speak in such a way that transformation in our lives truly begins. Because His edification, His answers, His comfort, and His counsel introduce disarming love. His dignity invites us to vulnerability, and, in the unseen place, He begins to slowly but surely spiritually undress us. It's there we also find the safety to explore Him, as well.

It's in the hidden place, in communion with God, that He honors our dignity by slowly removing our false identities, layer by layer. All we've hidden behind, all we've made ourselves to be, all we've crafted, and all the pretense we've carried. Layer by layer, piece by piece, He pulls back our façades, and by the power of His touch He breaks off their power completely. Moving at the pace we are willing to progress with Him, He dismantles all of the things we've hidden our true selves behind.

Unfortunately, our reaction as the layers fall off is often shame. As He pulls back our surface-layer sins, the process often makes us feel more and more vulnerable and uncomfortable. Just like many times, in physical intimacy, we insist the light be turned off or we quickly dash under the covers, it is easy to want to hide when more of our true, imperfect, wounded, and sin-riddled state is exposed.

But Proverbs 28:13 says, "Whoever conceals his transgressions will not prosper, but he who confesses and forsakes them will obtain mercy." Even our secret sins are exposed in the hidden place. Our stretch marks and sagging skin and imperfections and raw humanity are eventually unveiled, and for many that is too much to bear. But while acknowledging those pieces leaves us truly raw and bare, His gentle and patient disrobing should not be feared.

I find that those raw moments are when He steps back in honor and allows us to explore Him in exchange. He pauses to let us come out of hiding and back into the light. To, like Thomas in John 20:27, put our fingers into the place where the nails pierced Him and put our hand into His side. To explore His character and nature and be reminded that He is who He says He is. That He truly is safe and trustworthy and sure. And that "there is therefore now no condemnation for those who are in Christ Jesus" (Rom. 8:1), who walk not after the flesh but after the Spirit.

When we have undressed our presumptions of Him, pulled back layers of deception and manipulation we've draped over Him, and explored His dynamic nature, His faultless character, and His holy design, we find that we are standing, vulnerably, before the One who first made Himself completely vulnerable for us. We can stand unashamed, because He bore our sin and shame before we ever knew we needed His great love. And it is then, if we stay committed to the process of intimate exploration, that we progress to the point where our time with God is not just framed around frequency but around depth. Quantity and quality. The hidden places move us beyond just inviting to truly abiding when our heavier, harder, deeper layers of wounds and insecurity have been exposed.

He undresses our masks and false identities and hidden parts. Our disguises and excuses and unforgiveness and pride. Our pretense and our pain and our idol worship and our filth. And what shocks me—even still, time and time again, as I personally navigate ongoing sanctification with Him—is that He is not shaken by the rough state of my callous heart. He is not disgusted or offended by the imperfections of my flesh. He reminds me that He died to redeem them. And the Holy Spirit specializes in restoring us into the likeness of our Maker, somehow both instantly as well as one step at a time.

In fact, the gospel really takes root when we begin to stand spiritually exposed before Him and realize that not only is He not repulsed but He actually draws near, delighting in the beauty of His bride. Something about that kind of love—that kind of faithful, dignifying, stable, and illogical love—transforms something far deeper than our surface stretch marks and scars; it gradually transforms our hearts. This is the gospel of the One whom our soul was made to love.

And His love is a love that stays (2 Kings 2:6; Ruth 1:16–18). All of the gospel is revealed in intimacy that lasts, in the staying power of love. Just as Christ stayed on the cross rather than wielding His authority to bring Himself down, just as husbands and wives stick through the thick and thin of life, just as Christ remained by the well of the woman crushed by shame, in the face of the mess and the muck and the wounds and the worry, He is faithful to stay.

To know Him and be known by Him is to remain in His grace, under the shadow of His wing, and to know beyond a shadow of a doubt that He too will stay. The lasting power of His love and the faith to believe in that promise are ultimately the foundational pillars of the hidden place, and the true intimacy produced there is what sanctification is built upon.

Oh God,

What kind of love is this, that You are One who both listens and speaks? What kind of love is this, that You are One who delights in tender privacy? What kind of love is this, that You edify me with how deeply You respect me, how You captivate me with kindness and compassion, how You dignify me by revealing Yourself as trustworthy and sure? What kind of love is this, that Your unfathomable power is not intimidating? What kind of love is this, that Your inconceivable holiness is not elitist or exclusive but extended graciously to someone like me? What kind of love is this, that—in the face of my humanity—stays and rests with me? What kind of love is this, that righteously threatens to completely and regularly transform me? This kind of intimacy is different. And disorienting. Yeah, I just want to stay here awhile. To discern if this revelation of Your nature is true.

Speak, Lord. Your servant is listening. . . .

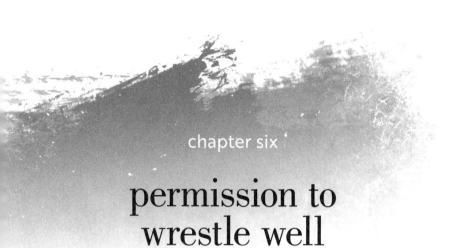

permission to wrestle well

There are a number of things that can keep a husband and wife out of one another's arms, just as there are a number of things that can keep us removed from true, transformational intimacy with God—knowing Him and being fully known by Him. While this list of idols, fears, distractions, and perverse emotions that contribute to unhealthy or nonexistent intimacy could go on and on, ultimately I see three large areas that inhibit us from experiencing what physical intimacy within marriage is intended to reveal about the gospel. These things are toxic to healthy marriages as well as detrimental to our understanding of how the Holy Spirit wants to engage with us, whether we are single or married. Again, we're just using marriage as a framework to help us understand His covenantal love with us by grace through faith.

The first of these three things, which we've already talked about, is our tendency to physically and spiritually slip into the darkness and hide under the covers due to *shame*. The second is our desire to *sleep* rather than actively engage. And the third is our failure to rightly understand *submission*, thus denying our partner or coming together only on our own terms.

Wake Up, Sleeper

Throughout Scripture we find the call to "wake up," "awaken," and "arise." There is a consistent, prevalent call throughout the Word for us to be spiritually awake, and that instruction came to life for me in a fresh way when I understood the call to intimacy by His Spirit. *Wake up, sleeper, and commune with the Lover of your soul. Wake up and be known.* I received this word from the Lord when I was processing the Hebrew word *yada* we discussed before and considering what it meant to intimately know God.

I was then pierced with conviction around the number of times, in response to my husband's kind and longing advances, I'd made the excuse of being too tired. I felt fatigued by the cares of the world and the busyness of my day, and though caring for kids and tending to the home and ministering to others are good and important things to do, the truth is I was still prioritizing the world and work above engaging with the person who loved me most, the one whom I had made a covenant vow to honor and serve and love all the days of my life.

The conviction seared deeper when I realized I was habitually doing the same to the Holy Spirit. Worn out by worldliness and the demands of this life and my own efforts, I was ultimately rolling over, asleep to God's kind and longing advances. I was prioritizing the demands of the temporary over the intimacy that cultivates eternal significance. I was truly and genuinely fatigued by life's demands—but rather than acknowledging Christ as Lord and prioritizing my engagement with Him, I remained consistently worn out and spiritually exhausted.

> I know all the things you do, and that you have a reputation for being alive—but you are dead. Wake up! Strengthen what little

remains, for even what is left is almost dead. I find that your actions do not meet the requirements of my God. Go back to what you heard and believed at first; hold to it firmly. Repent and turn to me again. If you don't wake up, I will come to you suddenly, as unexpected as a thief. (Rev. 3:1–3 NLT)

How often do we put up a front in our marriage that all is healthy behind closed doors, yet know connection with our spouse is lacking? How often do we put up a front in our faith that all is vibrant and intimate in our hearts, yet know that connection with our Lord is lacking?

We can no longer sleep. I believe God is calling His people to wake up from our spiritual slumber and draw near to Him.

> "Wake up from your drunken stupor, as is right, and do not go on sinning. For some have no knowledge of God. I say this to your shame" (1 Cor. 15:34).
>
> "Besides this you know the time, that the hour has come for you to wake from sleep. For salvation is nearer to us now than when we first believed" (Rom. 13:11).
>
> "Awake, O sleeper, and arise from the dead, and Christ will shine on you" (Eph. 5:14).
>
> "Ears that hear and eyes that see—the LORD has made them both. Do not love sleep or you will grow poor; stay awake and you will have food to spare" (Prov. 20:12–13 NIV).

The danger of remaining spiritually asleep and, thus, personally apathetic toward engaging with the Holy Spirit, is deadly. It inhibits others from hearing the gospel and experiencing the fruit of God through us, and it causes spiritual poverty—famine for our souls—rather than a harvest that yields abundantly for ourselves as well as for the blessing of others. Romans 13 indicates that the coming salvation drawing near as we await our Bridegroom's return depends on our willingness to wake up—to arise—to engage with the Spirit of God. To ultimately rouse and strengthen what little remains so that, like the five wise bridesmaids in Matthew 25, we would have our lamps burning and a vessel of additional oil ready as we wait.

Proverbs 20:12–13, above, is also clear that we are not just to wake up but to stay awake. Not only are we to arise and engage with the Lover of our soul, rather than allowing the things of the world to lull us to sleep out of His arms, but we are also to remain alert—to continue to invest, engage, draw near, and commune.

Entrusting All

> But because of the temptation to sexual immorality, each man should have his own wife and each woman her own husband. The husband should give to his wife her conjugal rights, and likewise the wife to her husband. For the wife does not have authority over her own body, but the husband does. Likewise the husband does not have authority over his own body, but the wife does. Do not deprive one another, except perhaps by agreement for a limited time, that you may devote yourselves to prayer; but then come together again, so that Satan may not tempt you because of your lack of self-control. (1 Cor. 7:2–5)

At the point of union, we are no longer our own. In the covenant of marriage, our bodies mutually belong to our spouse. The wife's body to her husband, the husband's body to his wife. And on the spiritual level, the same can be said of the Bridegroom and His bride, Christ and His church. His body belongs to us, as it was given for us fully on the cross, and our body belongs to Him, as we have committed to give ourselves fully to a life lived in surrender to the gospel.

The Scriptures clearly implore married couples to not deprive one another. To not withhold from one another. And they also give order and structure for intimacy with God—union with the

Spirit—to be carried out rhythmically and appropriately. I didn't understand this model for a while. Submission seemed oppressive and confusing when I simply read texts such as 1 Corinthians 11:3, "But I want you to understand that the head of every man is Christ, the head of a wife is her husband, and the head of Christ is God." What did that even mean? Then I read the following passage in Ephesians:

> Wives, submit to your own husbands, as to the Lord. For the husband is the head of the wife even as Christ is the head of the church, his body, and is himself its Savior. Now as the church submits to Christ, so also wives should submit in everything to their husbands. Husbands, love your wives, as Christ loved the church and gave himself up for her, that he might sanctify her, having cleansed her by the washing of water with the word, so that he might present the church to himself in splendor, without spot or wrinkle or any such thing, that she might be holy and without blemish. In the same way husbands should love their wives as their own bodies. He who loves his wife loves himself. For no one ever hated his own flesh, but nourishes and cherishes it, just as Christ does the church, because we are members of his body. "Therefore a man shall leave his father and mother and hold fast to his wife, and the two shall become one flesh." This mystery is profound, and I am saying that it refers to Christ and the church. However, let each one of you love his wife as himself, and let the wife see that she respects her husband. (Eph. 5:22–33)

It sounded so black-and-white on the surface. But when I began to connect the dots with regard to sanctification and intimate communion with God, I began to understand why submission is such an important concept we learn rightly. To not withhold or abstain but to submit. To not lord over or manipulate but to submit. To not deny or ignore but to submit—as we are mutually loved and cherished and provided for.

We aren't to deny one another but rather entrust one another fully with our bodies. Just as we aren't to ignore or avoid the promptings of the Holy Spirit when He stirs our hearts, convicts us of sin, or invites us to move in step with Him.

> Rejoice always, pray without ceasing, give thanks in all circumstances; for this is the will of God in Christ Jesus for you. Do not quench the Spirit. Do not despise prophecies, but test everything; hold fast what is good. Abstain from every form of evil. Now may the God of peace himself sanctify you completely, and may your whole spirit and soul and body be kept blameless at the coming of our Lord Jesus Christ. He who calls you is faithful; he will surely do it. (1 Thess. 5:16–24)

The Holy Spirit is on mission to sanctify us and make us holy. If we blaspheme against or quench the Holy Spirit in any of His many roles in our lives, we're forfeiting opportunities to know God and to be known. We're rejecting the invitation to join the very work the Spirit is on assignment to do in order to prepare us for the Bridegroom's return.

If we try to manipulate, withhold, deny, or control how and when God moves in our lives, we are only losing out on the fullness of pleasure and abounding love God is offering. We are not to deny the Holy Spirit's invitation to commune, and He assures us He will never leave us or forsake us, as well. True intimacy is cultivated when both parties carry the heart posture of "I love you and I long for you" and come together with frequency and with dynamic depth.

No, submission is not an oppressive command but rather the greatest call over the church. If all sin ultimately roots and originates around pride and control, then perhaps all of salvation roots and originates around humility and submission. After all, Christ our Savior lived a life of absolute humility in carrying out His call as well as completely submitting—or yielding—to the will of the Father in heaven, cultivated perfectly by His oneness with His Father. Perfect unity.

• ● ◉ ◉• •

When we look at Christ's mission on earth, we can understand submission more fully, as well. We often think of the term solely from the angle of oppression, diminishment, and perverse subjugation, but in truth, Christ's life shows us there is threefold power in submission.

One, the reality is that, yes, in submission there is always a layer of sacrifice and obedience that is tangible and dynamic. It subjugates our will to another's and is a denial of self. But who better to surrender our wants and urges and longings and will to than to the Maker of the heavens and the earth, He who is working all together for our good and for His glory? There is suffering and a putting to death of many things within us when we submit to the will of God, and sometimes this may not make sense to us right away and it may ache deeply.

But, two, can we not see that while there was surrender and deep suffering in Christ's life, there was also unfathomable power and purpose? Miraculous moves that raised the dead to life, brought sight to the blind, cast out demons, and ultimately unveiled divine power here on earth as it was in heaven? Miraculous moves unlike anything humankind had ever known? His submission shifted the course of history—what if the power that pulsed through us in yielding to the will of the Father could prove to do the same? To change the lives of those around us and see the spiritually dead come to life in His name? We often focus on the loss we assume is all there is to yielding and submitting, but I wonder if we would live more outrageously and powerfully for the kingdom if we instead shifted our focus to the unimaginable gain they can bring. In John 14:12, Jesus assures us that we will do greater works than even He. In my life, I have only experienced such power when I've yielded to the ways of God and submitted in obedience to Him. His ways truly are better than our own. If we exercise the faith to believe in this truth, yielding will always bear the fruit of spiritual breakthrough. It ultimately bends the knee to His power rather than our own, and His power moves mountains and calms the seas. His glory is above all things. Above everything. Most certainly and most powerfully above ourselves and our limited understanding.

Three, in following Him we may experience loss, but we also experience gain. And ultimately, the rhythm of navigating both of those things in tandem invites us into God's higher mission. Christ lived in submission so as to ultimately carry out the mission of God at hand. In the Latin root of submit, *submittere*, we see *sub* means "under" and *mittere* means "send, put." When we live in a submissive life in Christ, we too actively engage ourselves under the sending of God. Submission is an agreement to colabor, to engage, to commune with the General who has already won the war and who is inviting us into His greater story.

So, perhaps the power in intimacy is found not in denying the advances of God but in submitting to them, in not allowing pride, circumstances, worldliness, or our emotions to distract us to the point of concerning ourselves with the things of God only on our own terms. Rather, we live ready and willing, eager to spend time with Him and quick to accept His presence when He nudges our hearts. The long-arc linear curve of someone who is truly following Christ will not be one that ascends. Maturity, in the flesh, would seem to cause a linear curve that moves upward—that we would know more, have more figured out, be better, and need help less. But such a curve of ascension is one of self-righteousness. Rather, true maturity of the spirit is increased, reverent fear of God. It is increased humility and submission. Realizing, season by season, more and more, how desperately we need the grace and mercy of Jesus. With every revelation, we grasp more and more how little we knew when we thought we knew everything. How prideful we were when we thought we knew humility. How there is always more of God to know. And the linear curve formed with our lives in Christ is one that descends. More of Him, less of us. Death to self. Greater awareness of our need for God. The life of a Christ-follower will increasingly look like death at the cross so that we may know resurrection both now and in eternity.

If Christ's life demonstrated perfect humility toward, oneness with, and submission to the will of God—and it did—and we claim to want to be like Christ, then wouldn't our recipe for sanctification and holiness be humility toward, oneness with, and submission to God?

We must wake up from our spiritual stupor and stop denying the advances of the Spirit in our lives. Life is not about us. It is about Him. What an incredible invitation to submit and surrender to the One who is above all things.

Wrestling Well

When we refuse to hide under the covers or dodge into the darkness, when we refuse to allow the lull of the world to disengage us and coax us to sleep, and when we humble ourselves and refuse to yield to the selfish voice in us that wants to rationalize and deny our spouse's advances, there is a beautiful and miraculous moment after the undressing in the hidden place. A moment when two people draw together in a dynamic exchange. A moment of mental, physical, emotional, and spiritual oneness—an impassioned tangling of souls. An intimate wrestling match that begins in tenderness and trust. A labor of love that is both constructive and deconstructive at the same time. As this exchange builds in passion, it somehow, mysteriously, also tears down inhibitions, thoughts, distractions, and anything else standing in the way of complete connectedness. It leaves one breathless yet somehow also energized. Satisfied.

And it is simply a physical metaphor of the spiritual engagement with God we are all welcome to know, married or single. Young or old. New to the faith or mature in our journey. Because from the time we first come to belief, we all carry the same invitation to intimately engage with the Almighty. It is the direct result of resolving to come away with Him to the hidden place. Now, this is not a presumption that our time in His presence, our time in prayer, our time studying His Word, or our time in worship must instantaneously yield an outpouring of revelation, breakthrough, understanding, and transformation for our own gain. Rather it is an open invitation He gives us to slip away with Him and, in privacy and trust and ultimate security, wrestle with Him through anything and everything in our lives. Our sins, our unhealed wounds, our trauma, our pain. Our fears, our generational curses, our doubts, our shame. The reality of our emotions, our anger, our wants that contrast with His Word. Our wants, our questions, our anguish, our delights, our praise. He coaxes us in to become entangled as we seek His Word, His face, and His voice for truth and deliverance in the midst of navigating this temporary, fallen earth and the sin-prone body our spirit resides inside.

I think we're often afraid to wrestle through the tension within our spirits and through the confusing corners of God's Word and character because we lack true, deep, unflinching faith that God is able. Able to hold together His Word and His truth, able to defend Himself in the face of our efforts to unpack, prod, and explore His perfection. We, ourselves, are often fragile in our faith, so we've built a god of our own making whom we perceive to be as delicate as our own insecurities. We've learned the Christian language, we've modified our behavior to match the model of other believers around us, and we've sat silent and still in a place that feels "safe." But really, we're just marking time rather than engaging with the true gospel.

Christ died to bring the very divinity of God into communion with your soul. To ignite a flame of life within you that carries the power to cause wildfires of revival to blaze through every word you speak, person you touch, and place you inhabit throughout your days in Jesus's name. That type of majesty is stable. It is sure and steady and long-proven, like an unflinching fortress fully able to endure every assault and attack. Our wrestling with the details of God's design and the mystery of God Almighty is of no threat to Him. If anything, it is an opportunity for your own freedom, for strengthening your resolve and your assuredness of who God is— faithful, powerful, and mighty to save. The permission to wrestle well with God is a concept that permeates His Word. And His grace and compassion through the process are made clear to us on countless occasions.

We often mistakenly believe that bringing questions to God indicates a lack of faith, but the opposite is true. To bring the cries of our hearts to Him is the very mark of a relationship. To bring our requests and petitions and adamant longings to Him shows we believe He will be good to respond. He does not dismiss us for earnestly seeking answers but rather unveils Himself in the exploration.

Do we not see the very essence of God's heart revealed in this way in the Bible through the likes of Hannah and even King David? God marked these individuals as faith-filled and blessed even though in notable instances their humanity collided with His holiness through fear, shame, grief, and uncertainty.

In 1 Samuel 1, we see Hannah is desperate. Ashamed, frustrated, and fruitless. Likely feeling unseen and insignificant. Longing for the blessing of the Lord on and in her life but badgered by criticism, doubt, and discrediting fear in the process. In the midst of her discouragement, she steals away to pray and come into the presence of the Holy One. She prays in such a way that Eli, the priest, assumes she is drunk. When confronted she replies, "Not so, my lord. . . . I am a woman who is deeply troubled. I have not been drinking wine or beer; I was pouring out my soul to the LORD. Do not take your servant for a wicked woman; I have been praying here out of my great anguish and grief" (1 Sam. 1:15–16 NIV).

In her anguish, confusion, and bitter frustration, Hannah laments and cries out in vulnerability, surrender, and dire petition.

127

I don't imagine her earnest wrestling looked pretty or proper. Her posture matched the ugly and adamant words of a desperate woman. One insistent upon a move of the Lord, of a touch of His unfathomable mercy. A breath of His blessing. She became undignified and disheveled in her private and heart-pouring prayers. And "the LORD remembered her" (v. 19).

God paints this picture in a similar manner through David, as well. The psalms are chock-full of David's raw, vulnerable humanity. Fear, frustration, grief, anger, shame, joy, hope, and questions. Question after question. Anguish and agitation pour through these pages. But what is notable, to me, is that even despite his desperation, his pain, and his processing, David always ends his psalms in *praise.*

He peels through the layers of his God-given emotions—not hiding, stuffing down, ignoring, or self-righteously pretending he is without confusion—yet consistently ends in worship. Exaltation is the rhythm of David's words when exhaustion is on the cusp of winning out. He processes, and then by the stroke of his pen and the words of his lips, he reminds his own heart of God's rightful place—no matter if he better understands the intricacies of His ways or not. He consistently ends in a posture of reverence, praise, and submission.

Something about David's posture is deeply appealing to me. The ability to come before the Father and lay everything out on the table is disarming. God does not dismiss us for allowing our humanity and His holiness to collide. He does not punish us for petitioning Him with rightly postured hearts. Through Hannah and David, and numerous others in the Word, we are reminded that God does not admonish us when we lay our souls bare before Him. God counted these people as righteous, as noteworthy in His Word, even in light of their questions, struggles, and sin. Their faith was not dismantled by their honesty and humanity in the process of processing. In the same way, Adonai invites us to His throne room, yet He reminds us to come with great faith.

Hebrews 11:6 emphasizes, "Without faith it is impossible to please him, for whoever would draw near to God must believe that he exists and that he rewards those who seek him."

So just as it has stood for all of time, His invitation stands to wrestle, but to wrestle well. To dismantle and deep dive in exploration, but not to take the bait of discouragement. To bring our questions and our frustrations and our fears to Him, but not to allow the serpent's voice to cause us to question the Father's sure promises. To respond to the demons He points out in us truthfully, but not to cling to them because they are familiar.

Rather, we are to tie ourselves tightly to great certainty that He is God and we are not. And that He is faithful even when His response or timing fits a different mold than we fashioned with our own expectations.

We can come to Him like Abram. In Genesis 15, we see God making a promise to him, assuring Abram that He will give him a biological son in addition to descendants that outnumber even the stars in the sky. That despite Abram and Sarai's old age, God intended to make him a father of many nations. Genesis 15:6 reads, "And Abram believed the LORD, and the LORD counted him as righteous because of his faith" (NLT).

But two lines later, as God assures Abram He will give him land to possess, Abram replies, "O Sovereign LORD, how can I be sure that I will actually possess it?" (v. 8 NLT).

In a matter of breaths, Abram has been noted by God for his great faith and then petitions God for confirmation. He pivots from bold belief to a need for assurance. From radical trust to a prayerful petition for certainty. But Abram is not admonished for his petition; he is answered. With a faith-filled and pure-hearted posture, Abram was still human. And he earnestly wanted and needed the confirmation of a covenant. He longed for sure evidence that God's promises would come to pass. In our heart of hearts—in this faith walk we claim and the relationship we wrap our eternity around—don't we all long for the same?

Escaping to the hidden place and fully engaging with God is essential. We need to wrestle well. To ask questions. To listen. To repent. To respond. To cry out. And to decide we are no longer going to apologize for doing so. After all, 2 Corinthians 13:5 exhorts us to "Examine yourselves to see whether you are in the faith; test yourselves. Do you not realize that Christ Jesus is in you—unless, of course, you fail the test?" (NIV).

To know Him. To be known by Him. *Truly.* The desire to understand His heart must become more important to us than the desire to appear as though we have everything figured out. This is where true intimacy is engaged.

Abba Father,

You are mysterious, dynamic, and available. You are holy, perfect, and sure. Lord, I repent of my spiritual slumber, of my apathy, and of my worldliness that has kept me from communion with You. I repent of my denial to Your advances—for all of the times I have quenched the Holy Spirit by putting temporary things in my life above eternal things offered through You. I grieve the times I have ignored Your tugging on my heart and Your conviction in my spirit. I ask that You forgive me for the ways I have only come to You on my own agenda. Struggling to "fit You" into my life. Lord, please show me mercy and forgiveness. I thank You that You invite me to wrestle through the harder, deeper layers of my life with You. I praise You that Your grace is sufficient and Your power is made perfect in my weakness. Thank You for who You are as Teacher—that You stretch me, grow me, challenge me, and continuously call me to the fullness of my identity in You. You are worth the effort. Always.

Amen.

a deeper search for more

What is beautiful about the gospel engagement in our lives is that God, in His great and selfless love, always goes first. As 1 John 4:19 makes clear, "We love because he first loved us." This is the great and miraculous wonder of our relationship with Christ. Apart from His love, we do not know how to love Him. Apart from His great love, we do not know how to rightly love others. Apart from His great love, we live in a sin-bound and limited life. It is His initiation that frames the atmosphere of intimate gathering.

Christ initiates holy exchange by going before us and showing the way. Jesus told His disciples it is "more blessed to give than to receive" (Acts 20:35), and since we then "love because he first loved us" (1 John 4:19), we learn that in receiving from Him, we are compelled to give. This holy exchange between us and God, and then between one another, is key. It is key to sanctification and key, ultimately, to our activation by His Spirit.

The Father gave His Son, and we received the Word made flesh in Jesus. Jesus gave His life, and we received the great, saving measure of mercy, forgiveness, and grace. He sent His Spirit, and we received the powerful, emboldening, and divine presence of God.

He gave, and we received.

We received a pleasure and joy so great, we are led to model His nature and to give our lives up in response. It is here we realize we did not receive our lives to have them but to give them to the cause of Christ.

The same can be said of any number of things . . .

We did not receive time to have it but to give it to the cause of Christ.

We did not receive money to have it but to give it to the cause of Christ.

We did not receive influence to have it but to give it to the cause of Christ.

We did not receive a house to have it but to give it to the cause of Christ.

We did not receive talents to have them but to give them to the cause of Christ.

We did not receive a relationship or marriage to have it but to give it to the cause of Christ.

We did not receive a body to have it but to give it to the cause of Christ.

We did not receive gifts to have them but to give them to the cause of Christ.

Luke 12:48 says that "to whom much is given, of him much will be required." What I love about that verse is its inclusive commissioning to every one of us. Not just the affluent or scholarly or famous or seen, but all of us. All of us have breath in our lungs, life, and time—the most valuable gifts there are. Imagine if the entire professed body of believers surrendered every element of their lives to the Christ they claim to call Lord. Imagine if the gifts He gave us prompted us to embrace His greatest commandment, to love the Lord our God with *all*, and *all* is not merely received as a suggestion but a glorious invitation for those willing to die to ourselves. An invitation—and a promise that in death we find life.

So why do we, as Christ's bride, often let our wants, our will, our comforts, and our apathetic, surface-level faith paralyze us from responding to His advances of sanctifying engagement? If our life shows absolutely no response, on any level, in light of what He gives, then we may not yet know the full and transformational power of engaging with Christ as Lord. Rather, He is more like the celebrity we admire through our phone screen on the couch than the Lover of our soul whom we know personally and powerfully.

If our goal is to become like Jesus, whose life was not taken from Him but given by choice, we must choose if we too are willing to give our lives in response. Ultimately our lives reflect who or what they are lorded by. A good gauge on the maturity and depth of our faith is to ask ourselves, Are we willing to engage and surrender what is required?

This great exchange—when we respond to His sacrifice with our own—is where true holy work gains ground. Where engagement with Him moves from playful to passionate. From light-hearted to life-transforming. This is the great exchange that brings true *yada* to life.

Communion with God is about not just frequency but also depth. It is not just about continuously dipping our toes into the water; it is about wading into the depths and learning how to swim. It is not just about coming together regularly with the Lover of our soul; it is about the quality of engagement as we pour out our hearts to one another. Depth—and allowing Him to search and know, to minister to the deepest parts of our mind, heart, body, and soul. This is not always easy. That is why I believe Christ honors us by taking things slowly and waiting for us to acknowledge our deeper need for Him.

Revealing the Roots

When I found myself at a place of longing for greater depth of understanding and was willing to open my heart to whatever it was God pointed out or chose to reveal to me, He drew me to a hard place of recognizing that things in my spiritual life were not simple or single-dimensional. And, in fact, there were a lot of dark spiritual forces I was still allowing to inhabit my heart and affect my life tremendously.

For a long time, I dismissed that a Holy Spirit–filled believer could still have unclean spirits within them or a heart compromised by agreement with demonic forces. But this was a tactic used by the enemy to keep me immature and unaware in my faith. My progression in spiritual maturity remained completely stagnant and, frankly, coaxed me out of the hidden place—out of intimacy with the Holy Spirit—when I thought this way, because I did not perceive any urgency about seeking transformational intimacy.

When I finally acknowledged how spiritually dry I felt, God opened my eyes by His Spirit to the deeper, harder, more transformational work He seeks to do in us if we will yield. You see, when we're in intimacy with God—we resolve to truly know Him and be known by Him—He begins to unveil mysteries of Himself that help puzzle pieces "click" as we grow in faith. And His personal touch and tending to the intimate parts of our individual lives and unique stories make His love all the more tangible and real.

If we can agree that Christ was proficient in speaking through parables, and He Himself was the Word made flesh, we must agree that His Word is also consistent to His character and speaks prophetically to those who resolve to understand Him deeply. Deuteronomy 29:29 says, "The secret things belong to the Lord our God, but the things that are revealed belong to us and to our children forever, that we may do all the words of this law." So, those who resolve to commune in dynamic intimacy with the Holy Spirit, the One who reveals all things, are blessed with revelation of His heart and His heavenly design.

[Jesus said,] "Whoever has ears, let them hear."

The disciples came to him and asked, "Why do you speak to the people in parables?" He replied, "Because the knowledge of the secrets of the kingdom of heaven has been given to you, but not to them. Whoever has will be given more, and they will have an abundance. Whoever does not have, even what they have will be taken from them. This is why I speak to them in parables: "Though seeing, they do not see; though hearing, they do not hear or understand. In them is fulfilled the prophecy of Isaiah:

"'You will be ever hearing but never understanding; you will be ever seeing but never perceiving. For this people's heart has become calloused; they hardly hear with their ears, and they have closed their eyes. Otherwise they might see with their eyes, hear with their ears, understand with their hearts and turn, and I would heal them.' But blessed are your eyes because they see, and your ears because they hear. For truly I tell you, many prophets and righteous people longed to see what you see but did not see it, and to hear what you hear but did not hear it." (Matt. 13:9–17 NIV)

In light of these truths, I was forced to reckon with a lie I had believed for a very long time, a lie that said if I had the Holy Spirit, I could not have any other spirits within me, influencing my actions, decisions, and life. I often heard the common expression that "light could not exist with darkness." But I realized, as I allowed Him to stretch my understanding and dismantle my unstable arguments, that I was perceiving His Word incompletely because I was seeking to defend truth only by what my eyes and mind could perceive through reading the Word. I was failing to seek understanding in the Spirit. I had not opened myself to Christ's humbling invitation to take me deeper than I could stand. Deeper—to a place where I earnestly needed the power of His name to be my battle cry.

For a long time my understanding of sin and the dynamic spiritual realities at play in the lives of everyone—believers and nonbelievers alike—had been veiled, but I began to realize that my preference to remain shallow and vague in the spiritual fight for my life was the very antithesis of the power afforded me through the life, death, and resurrection of Christ! And my shallow understanding caused me to diminish the importance of humility and repentance, as well as downplay the matchless and perfect power of Christ—God's very vessel to bring the clean among the unclean in order to drive out and defeat darkness, to break the power of every sin's hold on my life.

Holy, by definition, means sacred, sanctified, and divine. Clean, pure, without sin. The Holy Spirit is the perfect and pure Spirit of God. And one of the primary works of the Spirit within us is to transform us, purify us, heal us, and *drive out* the very darkness that fights to hold ground in our lives. When we pursue and grow in holiness, we learn to yield to the Holy Spirit in order that access points of the enemy may be covered by Christ's blood, that trauma from our past may be healed and restored by Christ's blood, that habitual sin may cease by the power of Christ's blood. This is a powerful, progressive, and beautiful work of the Spirit within us, a work we also see progress through the New Testament believers from the book of Matthew through Revelation. All throughout the text, believers were rebuked for sin, corrected repeatedly by Paul, called to areas of repentance in Revelation time and time again, chastised for their agreement with darkness—and led in love toward the fullness of truth. Our humanity and spiritual depravity collide with the Spirit of God's righteous indwelling! Hence our need for the body of Christ for teaching, edification, encouragement, rebuke, and support. We need one another, we need the Holy Spirit, and we need His dynamic communion to help us in the process of knowing Him more and being made into Christ's very likeness.

In this process of revelation around my deep need for deliverance and healing, and the sanctifying work of the Spirit to be carried out within me, I realized what the Scriptures actually say is that "The light shines in the darkness, and the darkness has *not overcome it*" (John 1:5, emphasis mine).That, by the tender mercy of God, His light illuminates the way for those who sit in darkness, and *guides* our feet "into the way of peace" (Luke 1:79). John 8:12 says, "Again Jesus spoke to them, saying, 'I am the light of the world. Whoever *follows* me will not walk in darkness, but will have the light of life'" (emphasis mine). First John 2:9 says, "Whoever says he is in the light and hates his brother is *still in darkness*" (emphasis mine). And John 12:46 reiterates by saying, "I have come into the world as a light so that no one who believes in me should *stay* in darkness" (NIV, emphasis mine).

Notice I have emphasized words here that are active and engaged. We are to hold fast to the perfect light that will illuminate and conquer any and all darkness within us as we walk with Him, yield to Him, and allow what has dwelled in the darkness within us to be brought into His perfect, powerful, unfailing light. Darkness cannot exist in the light—which is *true*. This is why we must actively yield to the Holy Spirit and allow Him to make us holy. This is why we can trust completely that His power and His work within us are fully able to obliterate the power of sin over our lives. In Him, we wrestle *from* victory, not *for* it, by the blood of Jesus and the perfect power of His love.

The gospel of Jesus Christ, in His time ministering on earth and His time ministering within us, displays the *progressive* work of revelation and surrender. A progressive work of the Spirit to deliver us, purify us, transform us, and heal us. Jesus was holy, perfect, and blameless, and He came to dwell within darkness (the world). Sin cannot exist before the Father, so God descended into the darkness through Christ to defeat sin's grip and power over us. Christ stepped into darkness to drive it out. He then gave us His Holy Spirit to dwell within us and do the same to sanctify us. To progressively drive the darkness out by our faith through His grace. First Thessalonians 5:23 reads, "Now may the God of peace himself sanctify you completely, and may your whole spirit and soul and body be kept blameless at the coming of our Lord Jesus Christ."

We perform the active work of yielding our free will and choosing to abide and accept His lordship, so that His Holy Spirit can drive out the darkness. We partner with God to separate what is unclean from what is clean. But it is not as simple as just the Holy Spirit versus the flesh. "For we do not wrestle against flesh and blood, but against the rulers, against the authorities, against the cosmic powers over this present darkness, against the spiritual forces of evil in the heavenly places" (Eph. 6:12).

To state that the work of the Holy Spirit is solely to tame our flesh is a lie that stands contrary to Scripture. We are given the Holy Spirit, but free will is never taken from us. Through every moment of every day, we choose whether we will come into agreement with unclean spirits, the sin dwelling within us, or if we, by faith, will agree with the grace of Jesus and His perfect victory over Satan, hell, and death to defeat all of the spiritual darkness within us and make us holy.

Going Deeper

Deep intimacy with God results in revelation and humility. We must humble ourselves before the Lord and ask Him to give us understanding. At some point, in order to cultivate true intimacy, we must ask Him to show us what parts of our hearts have or are continuing to come into agreement with what is unclean within us. We must hold fast to humility in the process of being made holy, and we must allow His Holy Spirit to shine His light in the darkness and drive out sin from our lives that we may be sanctified and pure of heart before the Lord.

Otherwise we're asking Jesus to simply help us with the symptoms of our sin rather than allowing Him to break the power of our sin and deliver us from the perverse darkness in our hearts.

We must take personal accountability for the filth we have spiritually come into agreement with and the fact that we are professing Christ as Lord with our lips while still sinning. It should break our hearts as we grasp the degree to which we are blaspheming the God who loves us so.

We must ask God to reveal what is at the core of our struggles so He can shine His glorious light into the dark corners of our hearts and drive out what is detestable. And that hurts. It's hard. But if we are willing to believe He can do it, this wrestling proves profound in our spiritual life.

It's not always pretty—sanctifying love. The degree of humility required in true, vulnerable engagement with God is more than we can even know to ask and pray for apart from the intercession of His Spirit. *Yada* intimacy with God is truly intense and all-consuming.

We cannot resolve to be like Ahab who, in 1 Kings 21–22, lived in wickedness, then grasped repentance, but ultimately ran from the continued work of sanctification due to his pride. He lived in antithesis to the Word and heart of God, which compels us to not despise the words of prophets or seek only what makes us feel good about ourselves. Ahab sought only what edified him and assured him the outcome his prideful flesh desired. Though familiar with repentance, when purification and instruction came, he rejected the pain of continued correction and lived cursed in consequence.

Repentance is not a one-time thing; it is a humbling rhythm in the life of a Christ-follower. We must continually lay ourselves bare before the Lord so He can reveal to us the deep, hidden, entrenched sins that rob us of so much spiritual life.

If we disengage just as things are escalating in intimacy, we'll ultimately crawl out of the holy marriage bed before any breakthrough comes. And we'll live stuck in a cycle that wrongly perceives intimacy with God as something that only strips us down and leaves us empty. That only requires death and never sees the nail-pierced, talking, miracle-moving Christ who guarantees powerful, resurrected life.

No, the giving and receiving are a mutual exchange. God is working to achieve internal sanctification in our lives. When we humbly receive what the Holy Spirit is ministering to us, acknowledge it, and give it over to Him, He takes the ground that darkness and sin inhabited in us and occupies it with His marvelous light. He leads us to give up what is *not* of Him so we can receive what *is* of Him: love, joy, peace, patience, kindness, goodness, faithfulness, gentleness, and self-control. Wisdom, knowledge, discernment, healing, wholeness, encouragement, assignment, and destiny. Righteousness, humility, courage, and resolve. We are to be known so He can give us more of Himself that we might know Him more in return.

There is suffering in this process, and it is humbling, but under the shadow of His wing and surrounded by His great love, His yoke is easy and His burden is light (Matt. 11:30). He invites us to give up what was never for our best so He in turn can sow His seed of life.

> Humble yourselves, therefore, under the mighty hand of God so that at the proper time he may exalt you, casting all your anxieties on him, because he cares for you. Be sober-minded; be watchful. Your adversary the devil prowls around like a roaring lion, seeking someone to devour. Resist him, firm in your faith, knowing that the same kinds of suffering are being experienced by your brotherhood throughout the world. And after you have suffered a little while, the God of all grace, who has called you to his eternal glory in Christ, will himself restore, confirm, strengthen, and establish you. To him be the dominion forever and ever. Amen. (1 Pet. 5:6–11)

The Lord presses us to extract what is vile and promises to restore what is good. He does not leave us empty or exhausted; He is the giver of good gifts. He wants to give us more of Himself.

We must remember in faith, as well as in our prayers, what our intimacy with Him promises to yield.

We cannot conduct ourselves like those in Matthew 12:43–45:

> When the unclean spirit has gone out of a person, it passes through waterless places seeking rest, but finds none. Then it says, "I will return to my house from which I came." And when it comes, it finds the house empty, swept, and put in order. Then it goes and brings with it seven other spirits more evil than itself, and they enter and dwell there, and the last state of that person is worse than the first. So also will it be with this evil generation.

No, when we yield to Him, recognize, and repent, we must remember the great love of God and not simply leave our temple clean, swept, and empty, but invite an inhabitation of the Holy Spirit! Of the goodness, gifts, nature, and truth of our God. Though there may be pain in the cleaning process, we can remember the instruction to invite in the Spirit to fill us in response.

Just as Jesus instructed us to pray, we are to exalt the holiness of our Father in heaven and immediately declare His kingdom come and His will be done. In the same way, we can also declare the coming and inhabitation of His kingdom by His Spirit in our hearts.

When He points out our greed and we hand it over, we must also pray to be filled with generosity.

When He points out our pride and we hand it over, we must also pray to be filled with humility.

When He points out our anger and we hand it over, we must also pray to be filled with patience.

When He points out how we lie and deceive and we hand it over, we must also pray to be filled with truth and honesty.

When He points out our hate and we hand it over, we must also pray to be filled with compassion and love.

When He points out our anxiety and we hand it over, we
must also pray to be filled with peace.

When He points out our depression and we hand it over, we
must also pray to be filled with joy.

In recognizing what needs to go and inviting in what needs to
come, our mutual giving and receiving creates intimacy with God
that leads us in love and holy delight. He is not just stripping us,
leaving us vulnerable and exposed to the elements. Rather, He is
drawing out what is not of Him in order to clothe us in the full
armor of God (Eph. 6:10–18).

We give of ourselves, naked and bare before Him.

Put to death therefore what is earthly in you: sexual immorality,
impurity, passion, evil desire, and covetousness, which is idolatry.
On account of these the wrath of God is coming. In these you too
once walked, when you were living in them. But now you must put
them all away: anger, wrath, malice, slander, and obscene talk from
your mouth. (Col. 3:5–8)

So He can re-dress us by His redeeming and edifying love.

Put on then, as God's chosen ones, holy and beloved, compassion-
ate hearts, kindness, humility, meekness, and patience, bearing
with one another and, if one has a complaint against another,
forgiving each other; as the Lord has forgiven you, so you also
must forgive. And above all these put on love, which binds everything together in perfect harmony. And let the peace of Christ rule
in your hearts, to which indeed you were called in one body. And
be thankful. Let the word of Christ dwell in you richly, teaching
and admonishing one another in all wisdom, singing psalms and
hymns and spiritual songs, with thankfulness in your hearts to
God. And whatever you do, in word or deed, do everything in the
name of the Lord Jesus, giving thanks to God the Father through
him. (Col. 3:12–17)

And in this dynamic exchange, we find that we are known and come to know the One whom we love. "Put on your new nature, and be renewed as you learn to know your Creator and become like him" (v. 10 NLT).

When we seek first the kingdom of God and his righteousness, all of these things are added to us (Matt. 6:33). Our intimate engagement with our Lord builds to a breakthrough. Our submission makes way for His sending. Humility precedes boldness, as spiritual perseverance leads us into the revelation of experiencing His powerful glory!

The Breakthrough

In response to the progression of covenantal love—a retreat to the hidden place, respect and honor that cultivate trust, submission and vulnerability, an undressing, and an intimate giving and receiving that require engagement and effort by both parties—there is an experience that is hard to quantify. A great gift. A release that brings both energy and relief, joy and peace, pleasure and fulfillment. The colaboring efforts of the bride and the Bridegroom that ultimately satisfy.

The wonder of the empty tomb following the tension of the crucifixion.

The euphoria of the Spirit's strengthening following the annihilation of dark spiritual bondage.

The joy of the good fruit that is born following the godly grief found in repentance.

The warmth and reassurance of daybreak following the dark nights.

Why should we engage in the humbling struggle of wrestling with God, of stretching our faith, of exposing the sins of our flesh?

Our loving Father promises breakthrough for those who colabor—a surge on the other side of His sanctifying might.

I think often of Jacob in this regard. In Genesis 32:22–32, we can glean many incredible truths as we see the process and result of his resolve to wrestle with God.

> The same night he arose and took his two wives, his two female servants, and his eleven children, and crossed the ford of the Jabbok. He took them and sent them across the stream, and everything else that he had. And Jacob was left alone. And a man wrestled with him until the breaking of the day. When the man saw that he did not prevail against Jacob, he touched his hip socket, and Jacob's hip was put out of joint as he wrestled with him. Then he said, "Let me go, for the day has broken." But Jacob said, "I will not let you go unless you bless me." And he said to him, "What is your name?" And he said, "Jacob." Then he said, "Your name shall no longer be called Jacob, but Israel, for you have striven with God and with men, and have prevailed." Then Jacob asked him, "Please tell me your name." But he said, "Why is it that you ask my name?" And there he blessed him. So Jacob called the name of the place Peniel, saying, "For I have seen God face to face, and yet my life has been delivered." The sun rose upon him as he passed Penuel, limping because of his hip. Therefore to this day the people of Israel do not eat the sinew of the thigh that is on the hip socket, because he touched the socket of Jacob's hip on the sinew of the thigh.

First and foremost, let it be noted that Jacob's exchange with God occurred in isolation. After he sent his family ahead, the Word notes that, "Jacob was left alone. And a man wrestled with him until the breaking of the day" (v. 24). This intense exchange occurred in the unseen place, where Jacob was left with a marker—a touch—a humbling wound to remind him of his humanity, yet it was also a miraculous encounter of unwavering resolve. While made aware of his weakness through a sanctifying touch that humbled his flesh, he did not relent but insisted on a blessing from

God. In response to his resolve, God changed his name from Jacob (meaning "deceiver") to Israel (meaning "he strives with God"). I find it profound that it was his resolve to wrestle, his insistence even through the painful reminders of his humanity and the Lord's supreme holiness, that yielded not only a blessing but a complete shift in identity. A name changed through the glorious experience of communing with the One True God.

It is by the marriage covenant of His blood that we are justified, and in the unseen, wrestling place that we are not only sanctified but also receive tastes of what is to come—tangible encounters with His glory. Experiential waves of what it will be like one day when we are glorified in Christ forevermore.

The glimpses of His glory we can receive through this process of intimacy are almost overwhelming. These moments are the breakthroughs, the game-changers, the tangible encounters with God's greatness and love that write new identities over our story. In these moments, we progress from servant to disciple to friend to beloved to child of the Most High King. We increase our faith in our God-given identity. We persevere to receive the birthrights of our belief in our King, as His chosen and beloved children. We awaken to the truth that the righteousness of Christ is who we are, and we are emboldened to go forth proclaiming the good news of a very good, tangible, real, and holy God.

It is these breakthroughs in our intimacy with God that change our identity, unveil spiritual authority, and allow us to experience the beauty of His glory all around us!

◦ ◉ ◍ ◉ ◦

There are truly few greater experiences than experiencing breakthrough with our Maker. Suddenly, the return to the garden comes into clearer view. We taste and see what is good. We encounter the vibrance and fruitfulness of communion. We realize, ultimately, that it is worth it. It is always worth it. Daring to touch the heart of God and being met by His grace in the process is the greatest treasure and joy. To know Him more—there is nothing comparable.

I believe we are invited to wrestle with Him just as Jacob did in Genesis 32, to step into stretches of adamant persistence and prayerful petition—refusing to yield until God makes Himself all the more clear to our hearts.

It is wise to remember that nothing—no question, no cry—we can bring to the Father is going to knock Him off His throne. Perhaps you need reminding that you don't have to settle for sucking up your uncertainties for the sake of seeming like a "stable" Christian. It is better to wrestle—to excavate and disassemble and reckon with His Word—in full faith that God will rebuild what's been deconstructed on a sure foundation. In fact, it is the deconstruction and reconstruction that transform learned, regurgitated religion into heart-transforming, bold relationship.

If Jacob got a glimpse of God's face and a taste of His mercy after resolving to wrestle, then we must want the same. To insist on the blessing of comprehending His truth, no matter how challenging the process. Because if radical revelation can result from a wrestling match, then there is no place for apathy or self-preservation in the life of a Christ-follower.

Rather there is only invitation to wake up, engage, submit, and be sanctified. Glory is found in the holy marriage bed, and that exchange sows seed that brings new life.

Abba Father,

Whatever it costs me, whatever it reveals in me, whatever it pains me, I just want You. And I know Your promises are sure, that You will pour out the balm of Your Spirit over the places You remove that are not of You. That You are faithful to give good gifts, to bear good fruit in those who repent. In those who allow You to excavate in order to fill our lives, more and more, with Your goodness and Your glory. Thank You, Lord, for Your majesty. I rest in the truth that Your mercy is new every morning. That You are faithful, unchanging, and true. I praise You for Your perfect authority over any and all of the darkness that has rooted deep in my heart, and I profess with my lips now that I will resolve to stand firm on these truths. Lord, I long to follow You, to yield to You, to grow in trust and dynamic relationship with You. Thank You for caring so deeply about me that You constantly draw me deeper in Your love.

    Amen.

pregnant with purpose

It is not in vain, you know.

The vulnerability, the transparency, the laborious work of deep sanctification that mortally wounds our flesh yet miraculously revives our spirits. That invites us away from ourselves and draws us deeper and deeper into God's heart. It is not wasted effort or unproductive in nature. Drawing near to God and submitting ourselves fully to His holy love never leaves us barren.

God is not one to spill seed. We can learn from the story of Onan, in Genesis 38, that it is not in His character to withhold that which honors covenant, that which sows life, that which conceives the miraculous. He does not welcome us into covenantal intimacy just to use us, abandon us, and forsake us like the world does. No, He communes with us that we might freely surrender ourselves to experience Him and become impregnated with purpose and good fruit! Life lived in intimacy with God establishes itself purely and simply in faith, hope, and love. The greatest of these being love (1 Cor. 13:13). And love is cloaked in trust, in freedom, in transformational power born of His Spirit.

True intimacy with God is potent and proficient at bearing beautiful spiritual fruit.

He draws us into His presence that we may be fully known and, in turn, know Him more and more. When that invitation is accepted and the oil of the Holy Spirit is pressed out in that place, it is poured over us through supernatural anointing and stored in the reservoir of our hearts—our lamps. Then we find that, as with Mary, the Spirit sows seeds of life within us. For the Spirit who both conceived and was carried within Christ is the same Spirit who lives within us. Pause for a moment to wrap your mind around that.

Just as we are born of the flesh and must be born again of the Spirit if we want to inherit the kingdom of heaven, like John 3 explains, so too the Spirit seeks to conceive in us life and works that are not born of the flesh—of our own efforts, of our own timing and making—but of the Spirit. These works that are conceived by Him will one day stand when the refining fire comes to consume all that is false and burns up the chaff. Jesus said,

> Abide in me, and I in you. As the branch cannot bear fruit by itself, unless it abides in the vine, neither can you, unless you abide in me. I am the vine; you are the branches. Whoever abides in me and I in him, he it is that bears much fruit, for apart from me you can do nothing. If anyone does not abide in me he is thrown away like a branch and withers; and the branches are gathered, thrown into the fire, and burned. If you abide in me, and my words abide in you, ask whatever you wish, and it will be done for you. By this my Father is glorified, that you bear much fruit and so prove to be my disciples. As the Father has loved me, so have I loved you. Abide in my love. If you keep my commandments, you will abide in my love, just as I have kept my Father's commandments and abide in his love. These things I have spoken to you, that my joy may be in you, and that your joy may be full. (John 15:4–11)

This is one of the reasons intimacy with God is so vital: the only work truly considered "good" in the eyes of God is work conceived by His Spirit. Our good works—in our flesh, in our own efforts and attempts—are as unclean as we are. Polluted and filthy, "like a menstrual rag" (Isa. 64:6 NET). Communion with ourselves, trust in the flesh, intimacy with the enemy—all conceive nothing of eternal purpose. But intimacy with God conceives the miraculous. Good, fire-tested, holy transformation and fruit.

In intimacy with Him, purpose is conceived.

Joy is conceived.

Sure love is conceived.

Peace pulses to life.

Forbearance develops.

Gentleness gestates.

Faithfulness finds its legs.

Kindness kicks.

Goodness grows.

Self-control swells.

And against these things there is no law (Gal. 5:22–23).

In intimacy with God boldness rolls breech.

Praise pulses.

Worship is enwombed, a constant focus of our hearts.

Prayer matures.

Courage grows lungs.

Generosity rhythmically shows.

Forgiveness presses on every internal pressure point we know.

Radical, contagious life swells within us to the point that, just like a ripe, round belly on a waddling, pregnant mother, the fruit of our intimacy with Him cannot be hidden any longer but becomes the point of conversation everywhere we go.

As we abide in Him, and His Spirit conceives purpose and life in us, there is a real and tangible transformation both within us and without that the world around us can't help but notice.

In the hidden place, life is conceived, and we hear from Him directly. Our identity shifts. Just as a woman becomes a mother, so followers become faithful disciples as He conceives and develops the very assignment over our lives within us.

His assignments look different in different people's lives. And, through different seasons of life, He may conceive and bear multiple, diverse works of His Spirit in and through a person's life. He is sovereign, and He is faithful to cultivate what He intends in His right timing. Our invitation is to be available and faithful, to receive from Him and to carry the call into life.

Works born of His Spirit may look like assignments of encouragement, generosity, leadership, mercy, prophecy, service, or teaching (Rom. 12). They may be works of apostleship, pastoral care of others in your life, or works of evangelism (Eph. 4). They may be unseen and underpraised by the world's standard but deeply valuable works of service that require you lay down your life (1 Pet. 4). Prayer is one powerful act of service that comes to mind. Other gifts include administration, discernment, healing, tongues, interpretation of tongues, wisdom, radical faith, words of knowledge, and even miraculous moves of His Spirit (1 Cor. 12).

God has incredible plans and purposes for your life. He has work that He desires to assign to you and mission that He desires to set you out on. It is only in intimacy with Him that you can personally discern, by "spiritual ultrasound," the specifics and details of the call. But the joy of that miraculous gestation calls us forward on assignment. And it leaves the thought of "abortion," or abandoning the specific assignment God has spoken to your heart, inconceivable. To the one who has known endurance with the Lord through the highs and the lows, the one to whom He has revealed the very value of their life—His eager willingness to intertwine His divinity within it and His overwhelming offer to bear fruit in and through them to affect the hurting world—the thought of aborting that mission, of killing that call . . . well, it's simply not an option. Faith in Him is a willingness to, by all means possible, fight for that life. To fight for the cause of Christ. To fight like kingdom come depends on it and endure through the struggle of carrying and, thus, birthing His work to life.

Labor and Delivery

It's the labor pains that bring fear for most.

The labor and the pain of faithfulness here on earth are unavoidable in the life of a true Christ-follower. But we are often proficient at longing for spiritual epidurals, it would seem. While God's grace is intended to be the power source that enables us to labor well, we often pervert its definition into that of a sedative that ultimately leaves us disengaged with the process at hand.

Because the world has convinced us we don't have to—in fact shouldn't have to—ever feel pain, we often assume a spiritual elitism, as if we are above the suffering Christ assured to the church. But suffering is necessary to birth forth His will here on earth as it is in heaven.

After all, it was in the garden that, after Eve sinned, He told her (woman/the church), "I will surely multiply your pain in childbearing; in pain you shall bring forth children. Your desire shall be contrary to your husband, but he shall rule over you" (Gen. 3:16).

Our desire is often contrary to the ways and the call of Christ, but He truly is our Master. And if He gave us the ultimate display of laboring, of suffering, of laying down His life completely so that the will of God may be done, then we must hold fast to Matthew 10:24–25, which says, "A disciple is not above his teacher, nor a servant above his master. It is enough for the disciple to be like his teacher, and the servant like his master." We must resolve to labor well for the kingdom of heaven to be birthed forth in and through us.

I remember the radical, revelatory work God did in my heart as I prepared for the birth of my first child, and I resolved to experience the fullness of what was at hand. When contractions finally began and what I had anticipated, trained, and prepared for finally became a painful reality, I was admittedly gripped and scared. But I was reminded, in the early, fearful moments, that this labor pain was pain with *purpose*. It was not like the pain of a wound or a fracture, it was pain that was working in sync with the very body God had given me to purpose opening and shifting so that life might result. The pain was immeasurable but survivable. And with each contraction I was closer to birthing the very thing I longed to experience and see fully realized.

My labor pains were impossible and empowering all in the same breath (see Matt. 19:26). When every ounce of my body wanted to quit, I knew the battle was truly just against myself, against my own will. What God was going to teach me through the process was guaranteed to be worth the pain. By His grace I was stronger than the struggle at hand, and by His faithfulness there would be life yielded on the other side. Quitting was not an option.

We must resolve to the exact same in our faith.

In the seasons of faith when we want to just give up, when obedience to God's call is painful and feels like it may rob us of what we want on behalf of what we need, His best for us is oftentimes synonymous with the hardest thing for us. And the crowning glory only comes when we labor and "press on toward the goal for the prize of the upward call of God in Christ Jesus" (Phil. 3:14).

And we will cry—we will be forced to cry out in the anguish of endurance through our days. But when the promised persecution, affliction, and opposition come as we carry out our call, our very heart cry of worship has to be, *This pain has purpose! This pain has purpose! Your will be done!* And the posture of our hearts, as we hunker down and position ourselves for pushing forth His kingdom, must not be for removal of the pain but for refinement in the process: *Refine me in this fire, Lord. If You will not remove it, then by all means use it.*

That was the very heart cry of Yeshua in the garden of Gethsemane, as fulfilling His call forced Him to such a place that all He could cry out was, "Father, if you are willing, remove this cup [of suffering] from me. Nevertheless, not my will, but yours, be done" (Luke 22:42). And an angel from heaven came and strengthened him. Then, "being in agony he prayed more earnestly; and his sweat became like great drops of blood falling down to the ground. And when he rose from prayer, he came to the disciples and found them sleeping for sorrow, and he said to them, 'Why are you sleeping? Rise and pray that you may not enter into temptation'" (vv. 44–46).

∙ ◌ ◍ ◉ ◌ ∙

This brings us back full circle, to a degree, to Matthew 7:21–23:

> Not everyone who says to me, "Lord, Lord," will enter the kingdom of heaven, but the one who does the will of my Father who is in heaven. On that day many will say to me, "Lord, Lord, did we not prophesy in your name, and cast out demons in your name, and do many mighty works in your name?" And then will I declare to them, "I never knew you; depart from me, you workers of lawlessness."

You see, it is one thing to bear fruit but quite another to dare to reach out and touch the heart of the Father. To lay down your life and pick up your cross. To labor well for the kingdom in order to gain Christ. To forgo the running, the rationalizing, the perceived entitlement, the desire to live a comfortable life void of faithful endurance. No, there is no inheritance for the lukewarm. His letter to the church of Laodicea makes that clear:

> I know your works: you are neither cold nor hot. Would that you were either cold or hot! So, because you are lukewarm, and neither hot nor cold, I will spit you out of my mouth. For you say, I am rich, I have prospered, and I need nothing, not realizing that you are wretched, pitiable, poor, blind, and naked. I counsel you to buy from me gold refined by fire, so that you may be rich, and white garments so that you may clothe yourself and the shame of your nakedness may not be seen, and salve to anoint your eyes, so that you may see. Those whom I love, I reprove and discipline, so

be zealous and repent. Behold, I stand at the door and knock. If anyone hears my voice and opens the door, I will come in to him and eat with him, and he with me. The one who conquers, I will grant him to sit with me on my throne, as I also conquered and sat down with my Father on his throne. He who has an ear, let him hear what the Spirit says to the churches. (Rev. 3:15–22)

Philippians 3:8–11 reminds us,

Indeed, I count everything as loss because of the surpassing worth of knowing Christ Jesus my Lord. For his sake I have suffered the loss of all things and count them as rubbish, in order that I may gain Christ and be found in him, not having a righteousness of my own that comes from the law, but that which comes through faith in Christ, the righteousness from God that depends on faith—that I may know him and the power of his resurrection, and may share his sufferings, becoming like him in his death, that by any means possible I may attain the resurrection from the dead.

If we are not suffering for the gospel in some capacity—by some measure of sacrifice—then are we truly living in intimacy with the Lord? Are we truly living in oneness with the One who laid down His life? To know and be known—it is a narrow road. We must be willing to endure the pain of birthing forth the work of the Spirit, no matter what the cost. Jesus was willing, and we must be too. He says, "Enter by the narrow gate. For the gate is wide and the way is easy that leads to destruction, and those who enter by it are many. For the gate is narrow and the way is hard that leads to life, and those who find it are few" (Matt. 7:13–14).

So, "Blessed is the man who remains steadfast under trial, for when he has stood the test he will receive the crown of life, which God has promised to those who love him" (James 1:12). Just as the baby crowns at the culmination of the labor, just as the water bursts and the woman endures the sensation of the "ring of fire," so it is by faithful endurance in laboring well for the kingdom that we bear witness to the fact that we are born of water and born again by fire in the Spirit. That we are His faithful remnant who will wear the crown.

Stewarding the Gift

John 16:20–24 reads,

> Truly, truly, I say to you, you will weep and lament, but the world will rejoice. You will be sorrowful, but your sorrow will turn into joy. When a woman is giving birth, she has sorrow because her hour has come, but when she has delivered the baby, she no longer remembers the anguish, for joy that a human being has been born into the world. So also, you have sorrow now, but I will see you again, and your hearts will rejoice, and no one will take your joy from you. In that day you will ask nothing of me. Truly, truly, I say to you, whatever you ask of the Father in my name, he will give it to you. Until now you have asked nothing in my name. Ask, and you will receive, that your joy may be full.

A mother forgets the anguish of labor when life finally bursts forth. The final pressing forth of a child is indescribable . . . euphoric . . . a genuine experience of glory. When the glory of intimacy flows through her, the expression of that gift into the world is indescribable—for both the one who labored and all who drew near to the process and were touched by a miraculous move.

This is how the gospel flows through us, how the world sees the Lord's power. How we appear as a peculiar people in an upsidedown world that is desperately trying to manufacture its own artificial glory. When the work of His Spirit is birthed through our lives, people in our vicinity take notice. They are drawn into experiencing Him, and, in the end, all are left praising God.

After my second daughter, Asher, was born, the only real utterance I could release was "Praise God, praise God. Thank You, Jesus. Thank You, Jesus." I had no thought in the moment of glory to say, "Wow, praise my womb. Praise cervical dilation. Praise my core stamina." No. While all of those things, and all of my efforts, were critically important to the process, in the end they were not the elements my heart longed to praise. A spirit on fire for the One True God does not seek to praise the created thing but rather the Creator. For His gifts exercised through us are for His glory and honor and praise alone.

And the stewardship of those gifts—the parenting of the Spirit-born works in our life—is where the beauty of the two greatest commandments, to love the Lord with all we are and to love others as we love ourselves, are both truly fulfilled. Because in intimacy, in surrender, in sanctification, in the hidden place . . . this is where we come to know the heart of God. Where we learn, in deeper and deeper ways, His thoughts and His ways. Where we experience Him and radically come to know His deep, identity-shifting love for us.

When He conceives good works in and through us, faith with evidence of works in our life, that beautiful overflow of intimacy is for our neighbor. So we can love others as He has first loved us. So we can manifest His love to the hurting and the lost and the confused and the wandering. So we can be fruitful and multiply, laboring unto the Lord for the building of His family. His transformational love toward us and His gifts exercised through us are for all those whom our lives may touch.

To know God is to desire to make Him known.

Who, after all, bears a child within abiding, covenantal intimacy and then hides the kid as well as denies they are married? No, we share gladly the gifts given, and we boast gladly in the One who loved us and provides for us. He births works of His Spirit through us that we might fulfill the Great Commission. Matthew 28:18–20 reads,

> And Jesus came and said to them, "All authority in heaven and on earth has been given to me. Go therefore and make disciples

of all nations, baptizing them in the name of the Father and of the Son and of the Holy Spirit, teaching them to observe all that I have commanded you. And behold, I am with you always, to the end of the age."

While the works we do are conceived when we have drawn away from the world, with an ebb there is always a flow. With *being* is an organic and heart-compelled *doing*. A drawing in and a sending out that pulses rhythmically through the life of a believer. The enemy will work to coax us back to the brothel. Back to isolation. He will bait us with lies of disqualification, whispering that we are unfit to carry the call God has placed on our life. But we must, by His Spirit, resist the spiritual "baby blues" that threaten to isolate us from the very world we're called to share abundant, Spirit-filled life with.

There is a difference between seasons of private intimacy with God and prolonged isolation. Genesis 2:18 says, "It is not good for the man to be alone" (NIV), and Proverbs 18:1 says, "Whoever isolates himself seeks his own desire; he breaks out against all sound judgment." And while it is important that we recognize our need for time alone with the Lord, we must recognize roots of deceit that might make the difference between intimacy and isolation blurry.

We cannot isolate ourselves. It is not of God and, if we look to what lies under the surface, it is often born out of one of two things: (1) self-righteousness, thinking we are above everyone else and do not need others, or (2) shame, thinking we are below everyone else and are not worthy to be used for the kingdom, especially in comparison to others around us we see being used for His glory. Neither self-righteousness nor shame are of God, and isolation can grow out of both. We must be careful to keep in step with His Spirit so neither pride seeks to elevate us above God's other children nor shame holds us in bondage apart from them. Rather, we must rest in the truth right in the middle: that we need God and we need one another. That He loved us so we could love one another. That while sanctification and deliverance are crucial, so also are we to "keep loving one another earnestly, since love covers a multitude of sins" (1 Pet. 4:8).

Yes, we carry the command to be the church. To gather. To love. To serve. Hebrews 10:25 says we should "not [neglect] to meet together, as is the habit of some, but [encourage] one another, and all the more as you see the Day drawing near."

* * * * *

We also carry the command to go and tell. To share the gospel. To allow His power to overflow us so that others might encounter God for themselves. And while there are miraculous, faith-edifying, flame-igniting days in the journey of living a life on mission for the Messiah, there is truth too to the reality that in order to be a bridge to Jesus we must be willing to be walked on.

A bridge does not have the luxury of presuming who will trample on its back in the goings and comings of a world at war, a battle between the flesh and the Spirit. Between our wants and His will. At times the feet that trod our bridge with clomping boots will be those of professed believers, and in the same day it may endure the dragging heels of those lost and looking to wound others as they wrestle within themselves. No, our bridge carries no privilege, nor should it bear the weight of offense. It has offered itself as consistent, sure, immovable, and settled. Settled deep into the poured foundation of truth, with four pillars bearing all the weight: the humility of the Son, the authority of the Father, communion with the Spirit, and obedience to the Word.

It is not the bridge's job to make sure it is appreciated or to harbor resentment toward those who may vandalize or trivialize its purpose. Others may hurl every complaint and offense they can find toward the structure, but may we not forget that if the bridge were not present, their grumblings would only shift to the conditions of the ravine they would be facing. And perhaps if we abandoned our position they would never even attempt to cross—to draw closer to the King, to think deeply about things they maybe haven't before, like living intentionally in their purpose and position. Holding fast to faith when the culture opposes all that honors God. Pursuing Him personally, listening for His still, small voice. Loving others with an eternal mindset rather than a tiptoeing emotional fragility.

Maybe, in holding fast and sure, we are making a way for more than we know.

Only God knows for what purpose He has positioned us to serve, so we must all individually seek His will for our lives. We must seek first the kingdom of heaven—and not just say that we've sought it but then just do what we want. We must truly surrender to it. And once surrendered, stand sure. Stewarding the work He bears through us out of deep, humble, earnest love for the other image-bearing creations of God who surround us.

If there is any encouragement in Christ, any comfort from love, any participation in the Spirit, any affection and sympathy, complete my joy by being of the same mind, having the same love, being in full accord and of one mind. Do nothing from selfish ambition or conceit, but in humility count others more significant than yourselves. Let each of you look not only to his own interests, but also to the interests of others. Have this mind among yourselves, which is yours in Christ Jesus, who, though he was in the form of God, did not count equality with God a thing to be grasped, but emptied himself, by taking the form of a servant, being born in the likeness of men. And being found in human form, he humbled himself by becoming obedient to the point of death, even death on a cross. Therefore God has highly exalted him and bestowed on him the name that is above every name, so that at the name of Jesus every knee should bow, in heaven and on earth and under the earth, and every tongue confess that Jesus Christ is Lord, to the glory of God the Father. Therefore, my beloved, as you have always obeyed, so now, not only as in my presence but much more in my absence, work out your own salvation with fear and trembling, for it is God who works in you, both to will and to work for his good pleasure. Do all things without grumbling or disputing, that you may be blameless and innocent, children of God without blemish in the midst of a crooked and twisted generation, among whom you shine as lights in the world, holding fast to the word of life, so that in the day of Christ I may be proud that I did not run in vain or labor in vain. Even if I am to be poured out as a drink offering upon the sacrificial offering of your faith, I am glad and rejoice with you all. Likewise you also should be glad and rejoice with me. (Phil. 2:1–18)

Our intimacy with God will bless us so tremendously and unify us so powerfully to His heart that our intimacy with others will become right-natured under His truth. Because to know God is to love God, and loving God always, always, always catalyzes us to rightly love others.

My God,

I can feel the power of what You have conceived by Your seed. I can feel the life You have brought forth inside my heart, the purposes You have placed within me. Lord, just as You miraculously construct life within a mother's womb, so I pray You will continue to craft and create the fruitful works You are curating within me. Lord, I will not fear the labor. I will not fear the pain. I will not fear the persecution but will keep my eyes fixed on You, knowing Your heart for the least and the lost, Your heart for my neighbors and my friends. If one of the objectives of Your intimate efforts is to use me for Your glory, then I will resist the devil until he flees from me. I will not be given to isolation or disqualification. I will not shrink back from the call to die to self when I know the power of what You are pulsing through me. Lord, give me a spirit of Esther that would say, "If I die, I die." By her faith she was sustained, and many other lives were spared and blessed in her wake! Use me, Father. Bear fruit through me as I keep with repentance, and continue to bless me with the euphoric delight of knowing You more—of seeing Your kingdom come as Your power is born forth. Open the eyes of the blind; receive my prayers like a fragrant aroma of incense in Your courts. I love You. Please use me and help me love others as You intend.

Amen.

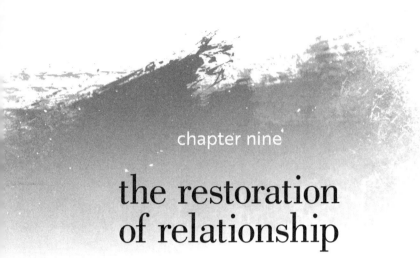

the restoration
of relationship

The Bridegroom is returning for His bride. Jesus is coming back.

The preparation period for ancient Hebrew brides was dynamic. And while the bride did not know the day or hour of her
bridegroom's return, she resolved to ready herself with full faith
that he would keep his promise. That he would be good to his
word.

The period of waiting was not without temptation, just as our
preparation and eager anticipation for Christ's literal return will
not be without struggle.

Second Peter 3:3–4 warns that "scoffers will come in the last
days with scoffing, following their own sinful desires. They will
say, 'Where is the promise of his coming? For ever since the fathers
fell asleep, all things are continuing as they were from the beginning of creation.'"

But we must stay awake, alert, hidden in Him with our lamps
burning. Holding fast to the promise of Isaiah 62:4–5:

> For the LORD delights in you and will claim you as his bride. Your
> children will commit themselves to you, O Jerusalem, just as a

young man commits himself to his bride. Then God will rejoice over you as a bridegroom rejoices over his bride. (NLT)

The spirit of the antichrist is at work within many, and those who don't know true intimacy with God will be lulled away into beds of spiritual adultery. What would result if the Bridegroom returned to find His bride—who was supposed to be set apart, sanctified, prepared, and awaiting His love—instead in bed with another? Courted by false idols? Intoxicated by the enamoring offers of this empty world and in violation of her commitment?

If Christ returned today, would He find you this way? Or are you intent on intimacy, seeking to know God and allowing yourself to be fully known?

If the earnest cry of our hungry hearts is a longing to be ready, to be made holy, then we must yield to His Spirit, obey, and abide.

Soon Christ will come for His bride, His church. Snatching her up from the world and saving His beloved from the wrath of God that will be poured out on all who remain unrepentant in their sin. All who have carried on knowingly sinning. In a moment, He will fully consummate the relationship by the revelation of Himself to those ready and waiting, eagerly anticipating complete and holy oneness with their Bridegroom. And the wedding feast of the Lamb will proceed—the great banquet celebrating our eternal marriage—oneness forevermore with our Maker. The garden restored in the new heaven and new earth, by His design.

Revelation 19:6–9 assures us,

"Praise the LORD! For the Lord our God, the Almighty, reigns. Let us be glad and rejoice, and let us give honor to him. For the time has come for the wedding feast of the Lamb, and his bride has prepared herself. She has been given the finest pure white linen to wear." For the linen represents the good deeds of God's holy people. (NLT)

God's holy people. *Holy.* Our lives must long for holy one-ness with every breath. Rhythmic, restorative communion that transforms our hearts throughout the course of our entire lives.

Is Holiness Possible?

Is it possible, on this side of heaven, to be made completely holy, as the Bridegroom so powerfully personified? Is the Author and the Perfecter of our faith able to make us perfectly like Him before we behold Him eye to eye? What does intimate oneness really stand to yield by faith through grace? If we seek to fully know Him, and to be fully known, can we touch the heart of God?

If we believe holiness is possible, we must also believe that it will not be ours by our own power and might, lest we fall into religious death—denying the Spirit in trying desperately to figure it all out by our mind, efforts, and flesh. No, if it is possible to be made perfect in the likeness of Christ, it would only be by His power—by living in radical and yielded intimacy with God who, in the Word, declares Himself both the Founder and Finisher of our faith (Heb. 12:1–2). Jesus lived sinless in the same flesh you and I are bound by and proved to us that He was able to do so by fully yielding to the Father by the Spirit of God within Him. If I dismiss the possibility of holiness for myself because it is humanly impossible, am I negating what is ultimately made possible through God (Luke 18:27)? As His offspring, as His child?

If we dismiss that holiness is possible at all, what becomes of our motivating, grace-dependent, urgent fight to the finish line Paul references? One that he perseveres toward so he will not be disqualified (1 Cor. 9:27)? If we set up camp in the thought that, ultimately, being made into the likeness of Christ is an impos-sibility, then do we fully believe the gospel? Are we preferring to rest in the fallacy of our flesh rather than rise to the power of the Spirit in us? Could it be that this thought of its impossibility has

167

been an open door for the enemy to use to progressively magnify the grace-abusing, justified but never sanctified, gospel-mocking infection of the modern church that has left us where we are now—"loving" God but never fearing Him? Acting in the name of God but never truly knowing Him? Claiming spiritual oneness but never becoming naked and unashamed before Him? Does it matter, at all, if we know the answer to the question at hand—or is it even the right question, after all?

What if living in the tension of the middle ground—the wrestling match of seeing the holiness of Christ and striving to be conformed fully into that image by yielding in intimacy to the Holy Spirit—is the very thing that proves our hearts as earnest, pure, and fixed on the things of God when we stand at judgment before the Father? That whether we reach perfection or not, our hearts seek first the kingdom of heaven? That our hearts seek first His heart? The enemy could not accuse us, in the heavenly court of law, that we were apathetic or adulterous. Double-minded or in agreement with sin. Lulled to sleep by a form of "grace" perverted into a sedative that ultimately yields godlessness.

Pressing On

I choose to believe, by faith, that all things are possible by God's Spirit. Namely because I know my flesh's tendency to be distracted, lazy, and easily deceived if I do not have a goal set before me—a focus my heart desires. And, in the end, it is not perfection I hunger for but to know the heart of the Father—His thoughts, His ways, His will—to know Him and be known by Him fully. If the journey of writing these pages has revealed anything to me, it's that it is always worth excavating the muck to rediscover desperate and divine love for Christ. The great joy of knowing and being known by Him—it satisfies.

Philippians 3:8–21 summarizes my heart posture well:

For his sake I have suffered the loss of all things and count them as rubbish, in order that I may gain Christ and be found in him, not having a righteousness of my own that comes from the law, but that which comes through faith in Christ, the righteousness from God that depends on faith—that I may know him and the power of his resurrection, and may share his sufferings, becoming like him in his death, that by any means possible I may attain the resurrection from the dead.

Not that I have already obtained this or am already perfect, but I press on to make it my own, because Christ Jesus has made me his own. Brothers, I do not consider that I have made it my own. But one thing I do: forgetting what lies behind and straining forward to what lies ahead, I press on toward the goal for the prize of the upward call of God in Christ Jesus. Let those of us who are mature think this way, and if in anything you think otherwise, God will reveal that also to you. Only let us hold true to what we have attained.

Brothers, join in imitating me, and keep your eyes on those who walk according to the example you have in us. For many, of whom I have often told you and now tell you even with tears, walk as enemies of the cross of Christ. Their end is destruction, their god is their belly, and they glory in their shame, with minds set on earthly things. But our citizenship is in heaven, and from it we await a Savior, the Lord Jesus Christ, who will transform our lowly body to be like his glorious body, by the power that enables him even to subject all things to himself.

He loves us. And we can rest in that love when we know Him and are willing to make ourselves known. Yes, many scoffers will come, but we can hold firm. By His power, by His great love, we can yield to obey and abide. As we develop the spiritual disciplines needed to cultivate relationship in the "meantime," we must also resolve to rest in our identity as children of God and remember that the Lord too will discipline us in our process of resolving to abide.

While that word, *discipline*, may seem off-putting, it is actually inviting. Hebrews 12:3–14 reminds us:

Consider him who endured from sinners such hostility against himself, so that you may not grow weary or fainthearted. In your struggle against sin you have not yet resisted to the point of shedding your blood. And have you forgotten the exhortation that addresses you as sons?

"My son, do not regard lightly the discipline of the Lord,
nor be weary when reproved by him.
For the Lord disciplines the one he loves,
and chastises every son whom he receives."

It is for discipline that you have to endure. God is treating you as sons. For what son is there whom his father does not discipline? If you are left without discipline, in which all have participated, then you are illegitimate children and not sons. Besides this, we have had earthly fathers who disciplined us and we respected them. Shall we not much more be subject to the Father of spirits and live? For they disciplined us for a short time as it seemed best to them, but he disciplines us for our good, that we may share his holiness. For the moment all discipline seems painful rather than pleasant, but later it yields the peaceful fruit of righteousness to those who have been trained by it. Therefore lift your drooping hands and strengthen your weak knees, and make straight paths for your feet, so that what is lame may not be put out of joint but rather be healed. Strive for peace with everyone, and for the holiness without which no one will see the Lord.

You see, discipline is different than punishment. Discipline corrects, it prunes, and it guides. In order to be made holy as children of God, we must accept the discipline of the Lord as we persevere and abide. We are no longer thinking like children, perceiving discipline as perverse punishment and missing the fullness of His intimate love displayed through the process of correction and cultivation as we are raised, strengthened, championed, and led by His Spirit.

> For we know in part and we prophesy in part, but when the perfect comes, the partial will pass away. When I was a child, I spoke like a child, I thought like a child, I reasoned like a child. When I became a man, I gave up childish ways. For now we see in a mirror dimly, but then face to face. Now I know in part; then I shall know fully, even as I have been fully known. (1 Cor. 13:9–12)

I want to encourage you now. As you process and press forward, stay. When it's easier to run, stay. Step into greater intimacy with God. Please do not delay. And while I could continue to work to wrap words and imagery, parallels and metaphors, around His great and glorious invitation to know Him and be known by Him, I know that it is His Word that does not return void, and brings the clearest truth to our days . . .

> Nevertheless, God's solid foundation stands firm, sealed with this inscription: "The Lord knows who are his," and, "Everyone who confesses the name of the Lord must turn away from wickedness." In a large house there are articles not only of gold and silver, but also of wood and clay; some are for special purposes and some for common use. Those who cleanse themselves from the latter will be instruments for special purposes, made holy, useful to the Master and prepared to do any good work. (2 Tim. 2:19–21 NIV)

> For the grace of God has appeared, bringing salvation to all men, instructing us to deny ungodliness and worldly desires and to live sensibly, righteously and godly in the present age, looking for the blessed hope and the appearing of the glory of our great God and Savior, Christ Jesus, who gave Himself for us to redeem us from every lawless deed, and to purify for Himself a people for His own possession, zealous for good deeds. (Titus 2:11–14 NASB)

He has saved us and called us to a holy life—not because of anything we have done but because of his own purpose and grace. This grace was given us in Christ Jesus before the beginning of time. (2 Tim. 1:9 NIV)

For we know that our old self was crucified with him so that the body ruled by sin might be done away with, that we should no longer be slaves to sin—because anyone who has died has been set free from sin. (Rom. 6:6–7 NIV)

Therefore, I urge you, brothers and sisters, in view of God's mercy, to offer your bodies as a living sacrifice, holy and pleasing to God—this is your true and proper worship. (Rom. 12:1 NIV)

Be perfect, therefore, as your heavenly Father is perfect. (Matt. 5:48 NIV)

Be imitators of God, as beloved children; and walk in love, just as Christ also loved you and gave Himself up for us, an offering and a sacrifice to God as a fragrant aroma. (Eph. 5:1–2 NASB)

It is God's will that you should be sanctified: that you should avoid sexual immorality; that each of you should learn to control your own body in a way that is holy and honorable, not in passionate lust like the pagans, who do not know God; and that in this matter no one should wrong or take advantage of a brother or sister. The Lord will punish all those who commit such sins, as we told you and warned you before. For God did not call us to be impure, but to live a holy life. Therefore, anyone who rejects this instruction does not reject a human being but God, the very God who gives you his Holy Spirit. (1 Thess. 4:3–8 NIV)

No one who is born of God will continue to sin, because God's seed remains in them; they cannot go on sinning, because they have been born of God. (1 John 3:9 NIV)

Therefore do not let sin reign in your mortal body so that you obey its evil desires. Do not offer any part of yourself to sin as an instrument of wickedness, but rather offer yourselves to God as those who have been brought from death to life; and offer every part of yourself to him as an instrument of righteousness. For sin shall no longer be your master, because you are not under the law, but under grace. (Rom. 6:12–14 NIV)

May God himself, the God of peace, sanctify you through and through. May your whole spirit, soul and body be kept blameless at the coming of our Lord Jesus Christ. The one who calls you is faithful, and he will do it. (1 Thess. 5:23–24 NIV)

Therefore, since we have these promises, dear friends, let us purify ourselves from everything that contaminates body and spirit, perfecting holiness out of reverence for God. (2 Cor. 7:1 NIV)

Everyone who has this hope fixed on Him purifies himself, just as He is pure." (1 John 3:3 NASB)

Put to death, therefore, whatever belongs to your earthly nature: sexual immorality, impurity, lust, evil desires and greed, which is idolatry. Because of these, the wrath of God is coming. You used to walk in these ways, in the life you once lived. But now you must also rid yourselves of all such things as these: anger, rage, malice, slander, and filthy language from your lips. Do not lie to each other, since you have taken off your old self with its practices and have put on the new self, which is being renewed in knowledge in the image of its Creator. (Col. 3:5–10 NIV)

Flee the evil desires of youth and pursue righteousness, faith, love and peace, along with those who call on the Lord out of a pure heart. (2 Tim. 2:22 NIV)

Formerly, when you did not know God, you were enslaved to those that by nature are not gods. But now that you have come to know

God, or rather to be known by God, how can you turn your back again to the weak and worthless elementary principles of the world, whose slaves you want to be once more? (Gal. 4:8–9)

◦ ● ◉ ◉ ◦

You were made to know intimacy with God.
Created to commune with your Creator.
Tuned to know the sound of the Good Shepherd's voice.
Designed to experience His dignifying touch.
And sculpted by Him to house His perfect and powerful Spirit.
You. You are who He loves. God has made a way for you to know Him and be known by Him both now and forevermore.

So delight, daughter. Be sanctified, son. Draw near to Him and He will draw near to you. Now. Allow yourself, now, to be fully known. Lie prostrate on your face before His throne. Find yourself familiar with His friendship and devoted to His discipline. Learn the sanctity of submission and the open blessings from obedience. Learn intimate, vulnerable love.

Isaiah 30:15 prophesies, "In returning and rest you shall be saved; in quietness and in trust shall be your strength." So draw near, commit to covenantal love, wake up from your sleep, and receive His Spirit. Allow His faithful work to be conceived in you and through you as you are made holy and sanctified. Become spiritually naked and unashamed before God again, and rest in His mercy, His grace, and His love.

Dare to touch His heart now; dare to know God and bare yourself to be fully known. And the day you stand alone before the Father will not be unfamiliar but rather the finished work of His great love.

And as we live in God, our love grows more perfect. So we will not be afraid on the day of judgment, but we can face him with confidence because we live like Jesus here in this world. (1 John 4:17 NLT)

Amen.

acknowledgments

To Jeremiah, Auden, Asher, Ronan, and the next "baby Aiken" on the way—well, we know the drill by now. More books and more babies seem to fall hand in hand around here. Auden, you grew inside of me as I penned *Wreck My Life*. Asher, you were formed together as I found the words for *Sex, Jesus, and the Conversations the Church Forgot*. And Ronan, God knit you together inside of my womb as I layered a portion of these lines. You're out now making messes and lighting up our hearts with your dimpled smile and doe-eyed gaze. The adventure it has been scribing my thoughts and escorting each of your lives into this world, in tandem, has been soul-shifting.

Thank you, my sweet kiddos, for enhancing our days and swelling our hearts and teaching us so much about what it means to love more like the Father. Thank you for giving Mommy brief moments to write and for understanding when I had to slip away to chart chapters and chase words. And thank you for trying your best to wipe the streaks from my office door where you pressed your slobbery faces up against the glass and stared at my fingers as they danced across the keyboard. I will always treasure these hard but holy, messy but miraculous, laughter-filled, PB&J with a side of breast milk, Candy Land–playing, tangled-hair days with you. You each are truly a blessing from the Lord—a reward from Him. I pray God's truth captivates your minds, Jesus's love transforms your hearts, and the Holy Spirit empowers you to lay down your life, pick up your cross, and follow Him. We are cheering you on!

Oh, and that "we"—that you and me, Jeremiah Lee—I couldn't do a bit of any of this without you. Truly. If our children one day have learned by example what it looks like to lay down their lives for the love of another, it will be because they've studied you. You are selfless, thoughtful, and kind. You are trustworthy, hope-filled, and encouraging. You are my best friend and the embodiment of strong, patient love. You are both brave and humble, leading our family with authority yet such gentleness. My goodness, you should win an award for how graciously you have handled a hormonal, pregnant, book-writing wife three times running now! That's a dangerous combination, and you have always carried it with ease.

Thank you so much for championing me through this writing process. And thank you for supporting me when I had to step away from this project for a season to simply listen to God and make room for some unexpected but profoundly necessary rest and restoration. Coming under your leadership and your love is my greatest delight. You make hard things simple by the way that you love. Thank you for praying over our family and the mission God is growing through it, over our marriage, over our home, and over our labors together as a team. You are an incredible gift, and one I do not deserve. I thank God for you, my only one.

To Brittney—I cannot adequately thank you for all you contributed to this work. You have prayed uncontrollable prayers of wild faith, you have fasted, you have relentlessly interceded, you have gone to war in the spiritual realm, and you have laid on the floor to play DUPLOs with my kids for hours on end so I could scribe pages and process revelation in the presence of God. Every one of those things has carried equal value in the kingdom, because every one of those things helped this book gestate and be birthed into the hands and hearts and souls that need its words. I believe there is a tsunami of kingdom come that will pour out over this generation in response to your unseen, faithful, and often painful work. (Seriously, sorry for all of those body-bruises my super-sized children have inflicted on your tiny frame.) So thank you for all of the ways you laid down your life to serve our family and the kingdom. Your labor was not in vain.

What I would give to get the chance to peek into the throne room the day you stand before the Father. What a joy it would be to overhear the King when He searches your heart and unveils to you the tsunami of kingdom come that poured out over this generation in response to your unseen, faithful, sacrificial, and often painful work. You understand the mind of God to a degree that continually humbles me and reminds me I still have so much to learn. Thank you for who you are and how willingly you allow God to work in and through you. For real, Miss Bent-ney. Thank you.

To Bill, Teresa, Rebekah, and the Baker Books team—I'm so glad we were able to partner once again. Thank you for taking yet another leap of faith alongside me and for helping this message find its legs. From start to finish, each and every one of you played such an important, unique role and did such an incredible job championing me and challenging me. Thank you, as well, for your grace and your patience along the way. I'm so blessed each of you has contributed the unique gifts, talents, and fire God has given you to colabor on this kingdom work. And mostly I'm just blessed you put up with my wild and dizzying antics through the process. Ha! Thank you!

And to my Abba Father, whom I've been so delighted to come to know all the more intimately through this season of life.

Thank You for being a perfect Father.

Thank You for Your matchless Son.

Thank You for Your Holy Spirit.

Thank You for the full and complete joy of Your truth.
You are righteous, just, powerful, and full of authority.
You are merciful, patient, gracious, and kind.
Your love endures forever . . . oh, how my soul better knows
that now.

about the author

Book #3 means "About the Author" #3, and I suppose I should be running out of things to say. But, in truth, the Mo who wrote this book is a very different woman than the one who wrote *Sex, Jesus, and the Conversations the Church Forgot,* and a far cry from the girl who penned *Wreck My Life.*

Sure, it's only been about four and a half years spanning the release of the three, but those few years might as well be a century of time for the One who, in only a breath, can grow us and heal us and reveal more of Himself to our hearts. And, in so many ways, it feels like God has transformed me by radical measure as I've breathed in and breathed out more of His truth over the last half decade. As I've learned to lean in more to His still, small voice and obey. As I've discovered the permission to dig deeper, wrestle through hard questions, and allow Him to rebuild that which was excavated from the foundations up. So, yeah. I am a different woman now. And I suppose that's at least one mark of spiritual maturity. I hope, at least. I hope that we would always be transforming—becoming less like who we were and more like who He is. Wiser, yet increasingly aware we have more to learn. Bolder, yet increasingly humble. Tougher, yet increasingly tender. I feel that. All of that. Like a fresh wave every day.

I blame motherhood for that tender part. Well, I blame marriage too. My husband, Jeremiah, and I have been rocking this teamwork thing for a minute now, and growing more in unity through every stage of painful perseverance and powerful breakthrough. Marriage is hard work, but man, is it holy! God's design truly is best. God's ways truly are sure. God's promises are so firm and faithful. It's an honor to learn more about the heart of Christ through the biblical model of marriage. Oh yeah, and it's fun to serve Him in the process! We get to adventure around the globe together and labor, side by side, serving the kingdom. We get to take wild and crazy leaps of faith that somehow to me, with Jeremiah by my side, feel more possible than my own courage can make sense of. We get to teach God's Word, see moves of the Holy Spirit, and watch hearts set on fire at the name of Yeshua. Oh, and we get to grow humans— four, so far, to be exact. Ever had a kid pee on every square inch of your lap while they were sleeping on a plane? Ever unpacked the gospel until you were pouring sweat, then stepped off stage and had a tiny human nurse with the intensity of a thousand vacuums? Ever seen your daughter's eyes light up as she watched you pray in a room and see the Spirit of God heal the wounded and wake up the sleepers? Because our wild and wonderful kiddos—Auden, Asher, Ronan, and "baby Aiken"—join us as we follow the still, small voice of God. And it's the best adventure. A multigenerational team on mission together. That's how we see family. And every member of that team has an important role to play.

On the other hand, if you've read *Wreck My Life* or *Sex, Jesus, and the Conversations the Church Forgot*, then you know full well the bolder and tougher parts of me have always been there. The feisty, the tough . . . they've always been there. I think what the last half decade has served to unearth in me is more of a reverent, steadfast faith that dares to explore the deeper, the wider, the greater of God that is always available to be sought. It's amazing how our boldness and humility mutually grow as we discover more about the matchless power of the Father. That call to die to self—it's not as hard as we once imagined. That surge of resurrection power He ignites within us—it burns past our fears with less effort as we earnestly long to see captives set free. We go from self-preservation to recognizing there is a rescue mission at hand. And we're invited to colabor alongside the King. "He must increase, but I must decrease" (John 3:30). That becomes a reckless rhythm the more we realize how great He truly is and how constant He will always be. So maybe that's what's changed the most since my last "About the Author." I sure hope I continue changing and growing in this way.

As special as it has been to see the messages of hope, transformation, and timely, Holy Spirit–led revelation God has given me featured on a number of different platforms, I've enjoyed seeing the fine-tuning and meticulous healing God has done within me even more so. I've been known by a lot of titles through the years—*New York Times* bestselling author, All-American athlete, LSU homecoming queen, eating disorder overcomer, daughter of a suicidal man, car accident survivor, wife, mommy. . . . But frankly, I'm steadily learning that the most important and telling title I'm privileged to carry is simply daughter of God. That's the one that's changed me.

Because all of those other titles and banners are just markers of earthly chapters that will one day fade and pass away. But *daughter*—that one shifts the focus. That one points away from me and toward Him—the Perfect Father. The Great Deliverer. The One who makes all things new. And stepping into the fullness of that title inevitably steps us out of how full we are of ourselves in any given season.

So, yeah. Daughter. Disciple. Servant.

Those titles do not contradict one another; in the most beautiful way they define one another. They fit and feel good.

A Holy Spirit–filled daughter of God who isn't afraid to speak bold, raw, courageous truth to a generation being crushed under the weight of their sin, their circumstances, and the lies of the enemy. A disciple willing to share the gospel with raw authenticity, compassion, and Word-supported revelation. One who wants to see the lost found and professed followers of Christ activated and drawn deeper and further into the glory of God. One who wants nothing more than to leverage my life to point to the cross and to encourage as many souls as I can to set their eyes, minds, and hearts on the One who took their place on it. A servant of Jesus Christ making my best effort to understand and teach His Word in Spirit and in truth, passionate about awakening others to the truth of God and the fullness, power, and active work of the Holy Spirit in our daily lives.

I guess that's me—the *now* me. The always-has-been-but-is-always-uncovering-deeper-layers-of-my-divine-design me.

Hi, I'm Mo. Thanks for sitting and reading with me.

∘ ● ◉ ◉ ∘

Now, who are you? I would love to hear from you and learn about you. How did this book challenge or encourage you? What areas of your life did these words speak into? Please don't be shy about reaching out. You can connect with me through any of the outlets below. And feel free to jump over to my blog to read more of my writing, watch some of my videos, and find out if I'm speaking near you anytime soon. Atlanta, Georgia, is home to our ministry, BOLDLIFE Initiative, and our family. If you're in town, come worship with us! Or hunt us down at a city park watching our kids face-plant off slides and things. Hope to meet!

Instagram: @MoIsom
Twitter: @MoIsom
Facebook: www.facebook.com/TheMoIsom
Website: www.MoIsom.com
YouTube channel: Boldlife Initiative

. CONNECT WITH .

Mo Aiken

🐦 MoIsom

📘 TheMoIsom

📷 MoIsom

▶️ BoldlifeInitiative

If you're interested in partnering with Mo
to speak at your next gathering, please visit

MOISOM.COM

Candid Conversations about Virginity, Promiscuity, and Everything In Between

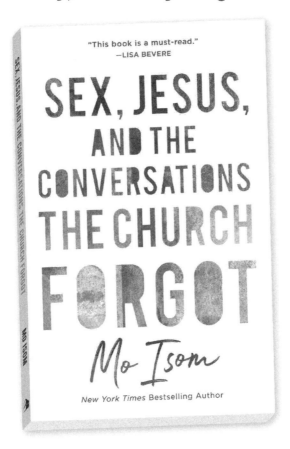

"This book is a must-read."
—LISA BEVERE

SEX, JESUS, AND THE CONVERSATIONS THE CHURCH FORGOT

Mo Isom

New York Times Bestselling Author

In a world obsessed with sex, why is the church relatively silent about it? While sex is twisted, perverted, cheapened, and idolized in popular culture, we leave young people drowning in the repercussions of misinformation, misunderstanding, and worth-robbing mistakes that could have been avoided.

Enough is enough. With raw vulnerability and a bold spirit, Mo Isom shares her own sexual testimony, opening up the conversation about misguided rule-following, virginity, temptation, porn, promiscuity, false sexpectations, sex in marriage, and more.

BakerBooks
a division of Baker Publishing Group
www.BakerBooks.com

Available wherever books and ebooks are sold.

Also Available from
MO ISOM

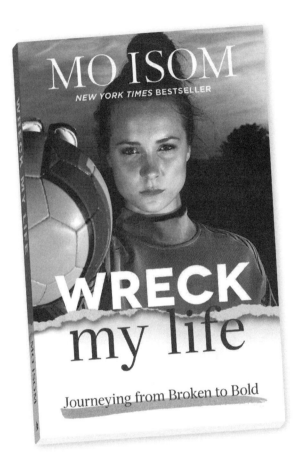

"Mo reminds us that brokenness is actually the very place God meets us the most, and the place where we can find Jesus like never before."

—Jefferson Bethke, *New York Times* bestselling author of *Jesus > Religion*

 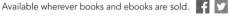

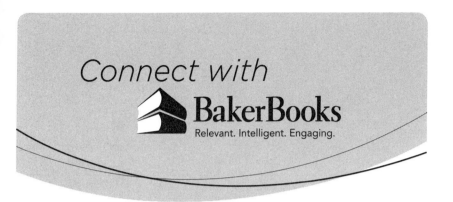

Connect with
BakerBooks
Relevant. Intelligent. Engaging.

Sign up for announcements about
new and upcoming titles at

BakerBooks.com/SignUp

@ReadBakerBooks